PRAISE FOR THE WORKS OF
REBECCA BREWSTER STEVENSON

"Rebecca Brewster Stevenson's writing is consistently powerful, complex, honest, and hopeful."
–Andy Crouch, author,
Culture Making and The Tech-Wise Family

"exquisite"
–Stephen Chbosky, author,
The Perks of Being a Wallflower

"A gorgeous meditation"
–*Kirkus Reviews*
(praise for *Healing Maddie Brees*)

"thought-provoking and sobering"
–*Library Journal*
(Starred Review for *Healing Maddie Brees*)

WAIT

WAIT

THOUGHTS AND PRACTICE
IN WAITING ON GOD

REBECCA BREWSTER
STEVENSON

Light Messages

Durham, NC

Wait: Thoughts and Practice in Waiting on God
Rebecca Brewster Stevenson
rebeccabrewsterstevenson.com
rebecca@rebeccabrewsterstevenson.com

Published 2019, by Light Messages
www.lightmessages.com
Durham, NC 27713 USA
SAN: 920-9298

Paperback ISBN: 978-1-61153-274-6
E-book ISBN: 978-1-61153-273-9
Library of Congress Control Number: Pending

Cover Art: Hilary Siber. *Further Up, Further In* [Oil on canvas, 24" x 70"]. hilarysiber.com

For Richard and Susan Brewster
my parents

INTRODUCTION

"Seek and you will find. It will be in His own time.
He is a lover, not a train."
—Peter Kreeft

For two of my childhood years, we lived in a small fishing village on the Japan Sea. Our house, along with the fifty or so identical houses in the compound, sat at the farthest reach of this village. My family had no car: bicycles were good enough to get us to store and school; my father, along with all the neighbors who worked at the Takahama Power Plant, rode the bus to work.

Otherwise, we went by train.

Even in 1977, a train could get you almost anywhere

in Japan. The lines were local and express, and if you wanted to get far especially fast, you could go by bullet train.

Almost weekly, my family and I made a trip to Maizuru. After the all-neighborhood Sunday school my parents held at our house, we would mount our bicycles and pedal the eight-minute trek to Takahama train station. From there it was a twenty-minute train-ride to Maizuru, where we spent the afternoon with some Japanese friends.

No one else in our little neighborhood of ex-patriots did this. Of course I can't be sure what they did with their Sunday afternoons, but I know I envied them. Not because I didn't enjoy the almost weekly jaunts to a city as comparatively large as Maizuru. I loved the automat with its egg-salad sandwiches and soft-serve vanilla ice cream. And I loved our friends in Maizuru: all of them English-speaking Japanese. Their traditional homes and storefronts and farm became almost second-nature to my five-six-seven-year-old self.

No, I didn't envy my fellow ex-pat neighbors their Sunday afternoons at home. What I envied was that so many of them—if not all—had their own car.

• • •

My family and I went everywhere by train. Several times a year, we made the trip to visit missionary friends in Kyoto; several times a year, we made the trip to visit missionary friends in Tokyo. And between these visits, we went elsewhere: Niko, Osaka, Kobe. We visited temples and gardens, watched ceremonial parades. My parents climbed Mount Fuji.

Train travel meant that, once we arrived at our destined city, we walked everywhere. We never took a cab. My little sister was still a baby, and she rode in a carrier on my father's back, but my older sister and I walked. I wonder how many miles we logged on Japanese terrain before we were ten years old.

All of this was fine. I didn't complain about the walking, because walking was how we lived in Japan. But I did audibly and many times wish for a car.

I don't remember how my parents responded to this, but I imagine cheerful indifference. A car, I can imagine them saying, was an unnecessary expense.

I actually enjoyed traveling by train. I grew accustomed to the rattle of the ride, if not to the rush and thunder that came with passing between cars in motion. The train stations, smelling of metal and cigarettes, were swept and accessible. And time on board the train was fun: our father read to us; we ate sushi from bento boxes; we colored; we watched innumerable rice paddies slide past the window.

What I didn't like about train travel was what came before it: the hurry, the sometimes running blocks of a town or city into the train station, the panicked delay at the ticket counter, the pell-mell rush down the stairs or through the tiled hallways to our platform where sat the waiting train with—if we were lucky—the doors still open.

Trains are always on time in Japan. I imagine it's a courtesy: the train says it will arrive at this time, and you will reach your destination at that time. It would be impolite—dishonorable, even—to miss those clear expectations. My father said it more than once of the trains in Japan: if your train is late in arriving at your platform, you are on the wrong platform.

Occasionally we arrived early to the train station. Weary from walking, we had nothing to do but wait. I had a lesson in time this way. It was late and the day had been long. I asked my dad how long it would be until the train came.

"About fifteen minutes," he said.

Mentally, I did that quick math. Fifteen minutes wasn't so long, I thought. I just had to count to sixty—relatively slowly—fifteen times. I sat on a bench and began counting. Four minutes in, I realized that fifteen minutes was actually a very long time. To a fatigued seven-year-old, it was tediously long.

Once we were returning to Takahama after a trip away. This was not our weekly excursion to Maizuru: we were in a town we'd never visited before, taking an unfamiliar route.

And this time we were late getting to the station. My father, with one sister on his back and other sister gripping his hand, was several yards ahead of my mother and me. We hurried after them, trying to keep them in view as we dodged fellow travelers. They reached the train well ahead of us. We watched them slip through the train's waiting doors.

And just before we got there, those doors closed. My mother and I arrived at the train seconds before it pulled away. I remember standing with my mother, my hand tight in hers, staring at my father and sisters who stared back at us through the glass.

We had no way to communicate; this was long before cell phones. Moreover, my parents didn't know if this train was local or express, or whether the next train would follow the same route. Would it stop at the next station, or might one of the trains continue on past several stops? And how could we know how to follow? If we took the next train, would the rest of our family be waiting in the next town, or would they still be traveling away from us?

A train conductor noticed our plight. I'm sure it was difficult not to: a family of *gaijin* among the Japanese, divided from one another by the closed doors.

In an act of kindness and likely unprecedented delay, the conductor pressed a button to open the doors and we, overwhelmed with relief, stepped inside.

• • •

Again, it was nothing about the trains themselves

that I wanted to avoid. It wasn't that I attached a kind of prestige to owning a car. I simply didn't want to wait for the train, and I didn't want the panic, the fear, or the potential disappointment that came with being late.

I remember saying to my father, by way of justification, of explaining why he should make said purchase: "You can't miss your own car."

I was always afraid of missing the train.

• • •

This is a book about waiting, not trains—or cars, for that matter. But if waiting is about control—or a lack of it—then so was my experience with trains.

I think children know a thing or two about waiting. I'm guessing you do, too. I've done a considerable amount of waiting myself. In fact, I am still waiting—and learning a thing or two in the meantime. It's those things I'm learning that this book is about.

ONE
EXILE

Nobody tells you when you get born here
How much you'll come to love it
And how you'll never belong here.
–Rich Mullins

We sat on the floor of my family's living room while my mother taught the lesson. She sat with us, holding up a poster she had made: a large drawing of a traffic light.

I don't remember what traffic lights were like in Japan, but a standard American traffic light would do. Most of the children in the room found it familiar enough that it worked as an object lesson.

My mother held Sunday school almost every week during the two and a half years we lived in Japan. I know that almost every *gaijin* child living in our small

1

neighborhood came. Once we had an Easter egg hunt. Another time we enjoyed root beer floats. I'm sure that, weekly, we sang songs and read Bible stories and played a game or two.

But the only lesson I recall is the one with the traffic light. It was a lesson on prayer.

God answers our prayers, my mother said, and he does so in one of three ways. Sometimes he says "yes" (the green light), and sometimes he says "no" (the red light). And sometimes—the yellow light—he says "wait."

Not a flawless metaphor, but even as a young child, I knew how to weigh some of this. "Yes" is what we're going for. To my child mind, it meant getting what I wanted. And "no" I recognized as the worst answer—with the degree of disappointment dependent on what one was asking for.

But what of "wait"?

That yellow light on my mother's poster surprised me. I was six years old. I can't claim much of my awareness at the time, but I know that I've never forgotten it—and I've forgotten countless Sunday school lessons over the years.

In truth, I can't remember what I thought about that lesson, except that the yellow traffic light—the potential "wait"—made God seem more real to me. He was not, after all, like the automat in Maizuru: a machine operating just outside my vision, dispensing responses based on my input and desire.

After that lesson, I knew that God was something more than that—something I couldn't see and certainly couldn't understand. But he was clearly something more.

• • •

I've never heard anyone say that they enjoy waiting. Granted, people might enjoy meaningful ways to pass the time. But the waiting itself?

I'm not talking about waiting for a meeting to start, a program to proceed, or a train to arrive. In each of these cases, the wait might be long, but it has an established end.

No, I'm talking about that other kind of waiting— the one with hopes clearly in view and no practical way of reaching them. This kind of waiting is an endurance game, its players charged with energy, passion, focus, zeal—and nowhere to put them. In these scenarios, waiting is readiness snagged on inaction, all interest and ardor curbed.

Normally, readiness precipitates action; to delay the process from one to the next feels unnatural, at best. It can be painful. And often, the longer one waits, the more difficult the waiting becomes.

What are you waiting for?

I have a friend who is waiting to be married. She isn't in a relationship; no potential spouse crests her horizon. But she wants that partner in life, that significant other who prefers her above all else. To reference the brilliant *When Harry Met Sally*, she wants a date on national holidays. Her friends are getting married, and her calendar is marked with bachelorette weekends and bridal luncheons—all for brides who aren't her.

I have a friend whose husband needs a job. It's been several years now of living on unemployment and any additional money she can earn by caring for other people's children in addition to her own. She watches her husband in a mixture of hope and sadness as he searches the internet and goes to interviews.

Once upon a time, I wanted to be pregnant. Meanwhile, it seemed like everyone around me was joyfully announcing their pregnancies. I likely bought a score of pregnancy tests over those years; my husband suggested we buy stock in a pregnancy test company. I admired friends' babies in person and in Christmas photos. I imagined what our baby might look like. Month after month I was hopeful, and month after month I was disappointed.

That's the pain in waiting: we see what we want, but we can't get at it. Something is in the way.

• • •

I'm thinking back to the traffic light, to the two *unpreferable* answers it might give. We can't pretend for a moment that "no" isn't the most painful. When God answers "no," a world of hurt is possible, with questions

4

and doubts rushing in that can occupy the rest of our lives.

But "wait" has its own darkness, doesn't it? "Wait" can feel like silence or inattention from God, and the lack of a timetable is agonizing. We might sometimes prefer a definite "no" to waiting's endless uncertainty.

My friend, a single mother, was going through a difficult time with her young son. This was years ago now, and as we sat together and watched our children play, she told me about their struggle. She put into words what I had felt countless times, and what I had heard so many other faithful Christians say as they waited for God to release them from their holding pattern and into that greener pasture just visible over the rise.

"I want it to be over," she said. "I just want to learn whatever it is I'm supposed to learn from this so that we can get on with a normal life."

A normal life doesn't seem all that much to ask for, does it?

Beyond the poster and my mother's instruction, I remember nothing of that Sunday school lesson when I was six. I don't remember what wisdom she cast around God's potential answers to our requests.

But knowing my mother, and knowing what I've learned about waiting over the years, I can guess she had something to say. I think she might have told us that waiting is worth waiting for. That my friend, who wanted to learn what she needed to learn, wasn't entirely wrong to say so.

• • •

Whether or not she was aware of it, my friend had already learned the first lesson of waiting. But this lesson is difficult to note, simply because it's so obvious. To the one waiting it seems less like a lesson and more a bald—and unhappy—fact.

How so, you say? Well consider for a moment my not-engaged friend who collects wedding gowns on Pinterest, or the twenty-something me squinting for non-existent lines on the pregnancy test. Consider again the friend mentioned above, who simply wanted to get back to a normal life.

The first lesson of waiting is that we are on the outside. We are separated—indefinitely and utterly—from that thing we desire.

Despite its being obvious to the one waiting, grasping it is also essential—less because it helps us with the wait, and more because the wait, whatever it may be for, is a metaphor: All of us are on the outside. Separated from what we want. In exile.

This might not *seem* true, of course. This actually might seem patently *untrue*. You might be happily ensconced in a loving family, a marriage, a tight-knit circle of friends. You might belong to a country club or a sorority, a church, a civic group.

But just as is true of those who wait, the human

condition is actually that of being on the outside, an unhappy state that poets have noted since the world has had poets. Exile is true of all of us, but we manage to ignore it with all manner of distraction: wealth and possessions, meaningful or frivolous activity, even what is truly good and beautiful.

The problem is that you can't contend with something if you ignore it. And this fact of our exile— the fundamental state of all human existence—is not going away.

Waiting can teach us this.

• • •

In July of 2001, we had three children, ages 4, 2, and 4 months, and the small start-up my husband worked for had reached the end. In the space of months, the significant investment the company had received was spent; there was nothing left.

They kept him as long as they could. We had watched in fear over the preceding months as one after another of his colleagues was let go. Daily we waited for the ax to fall in our direction.

When it did, there was no severance pay, no extending health insurance. The job-hunt my husband had already been pursuing for months yielded no employment and very few hopes—all of which, after months of conversations and professional persistence, dried up completely.

Two months later, the events of 9/11 had an understandable but terrifying secondary effect: hiring freezes everywhere. My husband's Masters degree in business from a top graduate school, his experience in international marketing, his practice in the world of current and rising technologies meant nothing.

Fear, in this context, was an understatement. How would we house, feed, clothe our children? How would we meet their needs for vaccinations and doctors' visits, those necessities even for healthy children at that age?

And despite being part of an economy in which this was happening to others, despite knowing it had happened to Bill's colleagues, we nonetheless felt very much alone. Occasionally we had reports of others' circumstances: so-and-so had found a job; this family or that was moving for employment; he was now working for this company, she for that. Over the ensuing months and years, the life-line that is steady employment—a given for so many—was never thrown our way.

Meanwhile, job loss simply wasn't happening to our friends or even most people we knew. I watched them with awe over things I had once taken for granted: a regular paycheck, the capacity to buy basically anything one was needing at the grocery store. Doctors' visits. Car payments.

We were waiting for a job that never came.

It works as a metaphor: We were a family of five. Two children by the hand and an infant strapped to my husband's back, all of us on a train platform. We were staring through the sealed glass doors at the passengers safely inside, and there was no getting in.

• • •

If you have asked God for something, and he has not said "yes," or "no," if you are among the loved ones enduring his seeming silence, if you are standing on a proverbial sideline or platform somewhere, then I am asking you to shift your gaze.

Don't stare at the train. Don't squint at the stick. And don't think for a minute that, just because I ask you to shift your gaze, the thing you are gazing at—the thing you want and are waiting for—is bad.

But there is something to be gleaned from the waiting itself—and this is what we must attend to right now. You are on the outside, looking in. But look around you. Everyone is on the outside, and this has been true from almost the very beginning.

• • •

In my most recent teaching position, my students and I studied the Genesis creation and fall narratives. Along with them, we looked at some artistic renderings of that early and pivotal moment, Adam and Eve and the forbidden fruit.

As you might imagine, visual portrayals abound. Michelangelo rather famously included this story on the

Sistine Chapel's ceiling. His tempter—half woman, half twining serpent—provoked a good deal of conversation in my classroom. We also looked an engraving by Durer, in which a cat makes to pounce on an unsuspecting mouse just as soon as Eve bites the apple. But perhaps my favorite in that study was the one that lacked these rich narrative details. It was Masaccio's fresco, a tall and narrow image entitled *Expulsion from the Garden of Eden*.

The painting is limited by its location, confined to one of several panels at the entrance to the Brancacci Chapel. As such, the artist included only the essentials to tell the tale. So we have Adam and Eve moving away from the garden, a space marked by the fronds of a single branch and a gate's arch. Above and behind them leans an angel, sword in hand, driving them away. During the Renaissance, worshippers at the Santa Maria del Carmine in Florence would have known the narrative at a glance: Adam and Eve, tempted by the serpent, have succumbed to sin and now are banished forever from the Garden of Eden.

Despite its simplicity, Masaccio's *Expulsion* provided us with good fodder for conversation. We talked about his use of light and classical representation of the human form. We noted the near-*contrapposto* of the figures in motion—that Adam and Eve are almost twisted in their posture. But most discussed were the expressions of pain. Adam's shoulders are hunched, his head bent, his face buried in his hands. In contrast, Eve's face is inclined upward, but her eyes are closed, her brow wedged in distress, her mouth hanging open. While other renderings of this moment demonstrate interest or fear, anger or shame, the dominant expression here is one of grief.

Which perhaps explains why it was my favorite among the works we studied. As one who had attended Sunday school my entire life, and as students attending a Christian school, we could sometimes neglect the weight of biblical narratives. But in Masaccio's skilled treatment, one can't overlook Adam and Eve's experience of loss. This separation between God and humankind is nothing short of exile. Here is the origin of that isolation and rootlessness common to human experience.

• • •

My students, astute observers and—most of them—fairly well churched, were quick to notice what they perceived as an error: Masaccio's Adam and Eve are naked. This works in both Michelangelo's and Durer's depictions, which portray the pair at the moment of the fall. But here they have been expelled from the garden. Why did he portray them in the nude?

Perhaps it was the influence of classical art. We also discussed another potential aim: their nudity figuratively emphasizes their shame and vulnerability.

But it reveals yet another important aspect of loss in this story.

When Adam and Eve were cast out of the garden, they were clothed not in the fig-leaf coverings they had made, but in "garments of skin" made by God. We get no further detail, but the underlying necessity is, of course, death: some animal had to be killed in order to cover Adam and Eve's shame.

And so here we see a further repercussion of sin: in those terrible moments of chastisement, the punishment falls on human and creature alike; both the people *and* nature will suffer: "Cursed is the ground because of you" (Genesis 3:17), God says. So the dust of the earth becomes the embodiment of death; the loss will permeate even the finest elements of the material world.

• • •

In many ways, nature rather neatly absorbs death itself, redeeming decay by converting it into fertility and compounding it to form coal; bringing new growth and life in the wake of forest fires, tsunamis, and earthquakes. But no matter your take on the story of Eden, the curse is evident everywhere. The earth, says Paul, is in bondage to decay. We see this less in nature's absorption of death and more in chronic flaw: distortions of how things ought to be, brokenness.

Beyond what mankind brings on through

exploitation or mismanagement, nature itself is embattled. Shifts in weather patterns—long before climate change—brought famine and flooding. As promised in Genesis, farming has always been subject to these challenges as well as to thorns, roots and rocks in the soil. But the problem is more deep-seated: the natural world meets corruption at molecular levels: an alteration in a single gene can shorten a life or encumber it with suffering. Diseases morph, vexing doctors and defying countless hours of scientific research.

Creation "is subjected to frustration" (Romans 8:20), Paul says. It groans.

• • •

So the Lord God banished him from the Garden of Eden to work the ground from which he had been taken. After he drove the man out, he placed on the east side of the Garden of Eden cherubim and a flaming sword flashing back and forth to guard the way to the tree of life (Genesis 3: 23-24).

Here we read what Masaccio illustrates: God prevents his beloved people from returning to the garden and, in the process, prevents their access to the tree of life. I wonder if there aren't two mercies here.

The first is stated. In choosing independence, humankind has chosen the way of pride and the self. Access to the tree of life in this context would mean the unbridled promulgation of that selfishness, which would mean eternal lives of struggle and despair. In this view, the flaming sword is protection: God protects people from themselves.

But again, I think there is a second mercy. For Adam and Eve—and all mankind—banishment from the garden means no chance to revisit it. Memory alone will inform our sense of glory lost and the beauties of that innocent place. Of what it meant to walk with God in the cool of the day.

When we are waiting for something—be it for marriage, a child, or a normal life—we can see what we're after. It's just beyond our reach, just through the train's waiting doors, if only they would open. But the exile of our souls is utter expulsion, wandering, a sense—if we are paying attention—that we have permanently lost our home.

God not only shut us out, but he shut us *away* from Eden, and this was mercy. It might be a terrible thing to be able to come close, to walk to the proverbial fence of that long-lost garden, to see how beautiful it is, to observe with the naked eye all that we have given away.

• • •

Charles Tomlinson's poem "Eden" begins with a startling claim: that he has seen the garden with his own eyes. But he is a poet. He can see things we can't; he can use concrete language to solidify the ephemeral.

Nonetheless, even in his view Eden remains elusive. It is the "light of a place" in addition to a place; it is a facial expression as well as the face itself; it is a gift, but one that has been taken back again. Half of his descriptors are not fixed, and neither, of course, is the wind that seems to give the garden shape, moving among its trees.

In fact, the second half of the poem illustrates our mutual expulsion, the exile that waiting teaches. Each of us, whether or not we know it, is "lost in the streets of our dispossession," he says. That we wait for return, that we desire a home, might be, in Tomlinson's view, both inevitable and hopeless. "There is... no way But the will to wish back Eden, this leaning To stand against the persuasions of a wind That rings with its meaninglessness where it sang its meaning."

Tomlinson's Eden is beautiful. It is a place of light and wind, a broad skyed garden overhung with racing clouds. And it is utterly inaccessible.

Meanwhile, we trudge under the weight of our "sorry roofs," rootless and dispossessed. If Eden does not exist, or if we can't make our way back to it, then where is home?

TWO
HOME

At present we are on the outside of the world, the wrong side of the door. We discern the freshness and purity of the morning, but they do not make us fresh and pure. We cannot mingle with the splendours we see. But all the pages of the New Testament are rustling with the rumor that it will not always be so. Someday, God willing, we shall get 'in.'

–C.S. Lewis, "The Weight of Glory"

I fear I have discouraged you. Rather than commiserating with your wait, I have asked you to look beyond it. Instead of making space for you to grieve your lack, I have asked that you see it as a metaphor. And rather than grieving the singularity of your need, I have told you that everyone is waiting for something: each of us is in exile.

In light of these failings, I hope this chapter's title

is of some encouragement to you. At the very least—as you can see—I haven't saved it for the end of the book.

I couldn't save it, because it's too important. Waiting teaches us our exile—a reality that those who *aren't* waiting might readily overlook. But once you know you are in exile, then you need to know the way home.

• • •

Robin had been teaching school in Durham for ten years when she decided to move to Ukraine. For some time, her church had been sending missions teams there; she herself had been among them for short trips during the summers. After years of thinking and praying about going to the mission field, she knew the time had come.

But despite having visited several times, knowing people there before she arrived, and feeling secure in her sense of calling, Robin found living in Ukraine difficult. It was in every way a foreign country, replete with strange customs, new foods and new faces. She worked hard at learning Russian, and while these efforts helped her relationships, they also reinforced the very real sense that Ukraine was not her home.

She missed the church community she had left behind, a tight-knit group of friends with whom she had shared her life and lunch on Sunday afternoons. Facebook and Skype enabled her to maintain these friendships and her sense of connection. She reveled in these and any opportunities to speak English: just the comfort of her native tongue made her feel better connected to home.

And then she came back—after three years—on furlough for a time before once again returning to Ukraine. She couldn't wait to be back in Durham again because while Ukraine was her mission field, Durham was home. She eagerly anticipated seeing her friends and being once more among the church community that had nurtured her all those years. She admits that, as a missionary returning from three years in the field, as a long-gone member of a community she loved, she anticipated some celebration.

People were glad to see her and were welcoming, but the celebration never happened. The church was still there, as were some friends and familiar faces, but other friends had moved away, and people had moved on with their lives. In many ways, the home that Robin had remembered, loved and longed for no longer existed.

Meanwhile, she also found that three years in Ukraine had done its work in her soul. She missed it there, too: the friends, the church, the sweet and unique details of the world where she had forged a new life. And yet she knew that being in Ukraine was difficult and still foreign in many ways. It was not home.

Which meant, Robin realized, that she was homeless: a comfortless thought. A home *is* comfort, she says, and also the root of one's identity. No matter where one goes, home provides a constant, a metaphorical foothold even if one's literal feet are unsteady on foreign soil.

• • •

The Bible's big book about home-going is Exodus, but Genesis relates some tales about it, too, one of which is the life of Abraham. The father of Israel is plucked from his home and obscurity to become the nation through whom God will bless the world. And it all begins, of course, with leaving home.

The Lord had said to Abram, 'Leave your country, your people and your father's household and go to the land I will show you.' So Abram left, as the Lord had told him; and Lot went with him. Abram was seventy-five years old when he set out from Haran. He took his wife Sarai, his nephew Lot, all the possessions they had accumulated and the people they had acquired in Haran, and they set out for the land of Canaan, and they arrived there (Genesis 12: 1, 4-6).

I think one generally prefers, when leaving everything one knows and moving to a new destination, to have some idea of what that destination will be, of how long it will take to get there, of what one might encounter along the way.

But Abraham's journey will not be a quick trip by car or train. The movers will not be coming to pack and then load those accumulated possessions into a eighteen-wheel truck. This is travel in the ancient world, along the margin of windblown desert, on foot or by mule and in either case a slow process. At a good clip, you might manage ten to twenty miles a day. But again, as you don't know where you're headed, it's impossible to guess how long this will take.

Moreover, this is travel in what appears to have been inhospitable territory—if not due to terrain, then certainly to inhabitants. This stretch of fertile land was dotted with small kingdoms governed by warring rulers who might carry you or someone you love into captivity.

So the move itself was difficult, but for Abraham there was more at stake. In making this command, God deliberately seems to wrest from him any sense of identity that he otherwise might have maintained: "Leave your country, your people, and your father's household," God says. In that ancient culture, Abraham's identity was bound in these things precisely. He was the son of Terah, and they lived in Haran; father and son had come together out of Ur. Abraham's inheritance, and therefore his future security, would come at Terah's death and would be part of the legacy that Abraham would pass on to his children, securing his name among them for generations.

Here, God calls him to abandon all of it for a destination unnamed. Abraham steps out of Haran and simultaneously severs all ties with his past and predictable future. Home, that metaphorical foothold, is abandoned.

Abraham leaves— and in so doing has cast his lot, pitched his tent, planted his hope in a God rich in power and promise, but One he knows only by faith. Like Adam and Eve, he is uprooted and sent into the unknown.

But unlike the cast-out Adam and Eve, Abraham walks toward the God who calls him, not away.

• • •

I've heard people speak of "home" in metaphorical ways. For example, I've heard a person call another person their "home." Or a family can feel like home. Home can be a town or a neighborhood. Or it can mean the more traditional sense of the word, the structure or space in which you live and are shaped by your family and daily experience.

It looks a little bit different to everyone.

• • •

The subject line of the email: "Stony Brook House," and the text was limited. Just a note from my dad, how pleased my parents were to come across the floor plan of the house my grandparents built in 1960.

I think they lived there for a little more than a decade. By the time I was six, they had sold it. They had their apartment in the city and the house where my parents live now, the one we return to every summer, the one "Out East," we say, at the almost very end of

Long Island.

But some of my earliest memories are from the Stony Brook House, and although the image in the email was merely a floor plan, just a map drawn up in pencil, I recognized each room immediately.

I was alone in my house when I saw it, but I think I gasped aloud. I looked down at a two-dimension drawing on the flat screen of my cell phone, but what I saw somehow was the full house, upright, entire. Room for room, closet, bathroom, window. The yard, the front porch, the smell of the boxwood out front, and the way the sunlight came into the rooms.

• • •

Lisa grew up just outside of D.C. Her house was a split level with columns across the front on a lot marked with grand old trees. She moved there with her family when she was two and called that house home through her college years. Now in her early forties, she and her siblings last year completed a difficult if not-uncommon task: they helped their aging parents sort through a lifetime of things, gather up what they needed, and move closer to family.

The house quickly sold to some people from Boston. They bought it without seeing it first-hand, via website and an obliging realtor. It fetched an excellent price.

Recently, Lisa told me she'd had news of that house: it's gone. They razed it. Not just the house, but the entire property: the trees and all the grass. So it wasn't the house the buyers were after, apparently. It was the lot.

That is, of course, their prerogative.

But just yesterday, Lisa mentioned it to me again in passing. Just a quick comment that opened a view onto loss. "I've known the house is gone for a month now," she said. And she has a full life here in North Carolina: a lovely home of her own, a thriving marriage, three beautiful children. But the empty lot reported by her sister is nonetheless on her mind. "I've known the house is gone for a month now," she said. "I'm still sad."

• • •

My sister and her husband have a large, old house in the country in western Massachusetts. It's set back from the road; you have to know where to look, when passing, to see one ivory peak under the roof and a window next to the chimney.

It was built in 1922 and is quietly grand: warm wood floors; glass doorknobs; built-in bookcases and a broad staircase, with landing, that descends into a generous center hall.

It has a second staircase that goes to what might have been servants' quarters, but if the house ever enjoyed that kind of exalted service, it's long lost to memory. My sister and her husband bought the house nearly ten years ago from a widow who had lived there alone for a long time.

But one afternoon, not long after they moved in, my sister found herself with smiling and unexpected guests in the driveway. It was a woman with her grown daughter, and the woman explained that she had grown up in that house, perhaps forty years before.

Together they walked through the rooms, the woman recalling to her daughter and my sister how her family had lived in those spaces. This had been her brother's room; here they had done their homework. This was where her mother kept the sewing machine, and they would talk together while they did their school work and she sewed. And on Christmas mornings, she and her siblings stood like this on the staircase, waiting for their parents to call them into the living room, with the fireplace blazing to warm the room, to the Christmas tree and the presents.

• • •

Abraham was seventy-five and Sarai his wife was sixty-five when they left home. Their journey was about 500 miles long. The packing and unpacking of supplies, the collapsing and pitching of tents were relentlessly necessary. And the travel itself was undoubtedly complicated by their large numbers: Abraham's possessions likely included servants, slaves, flocks and herds.

The process of traveling under these conditions

would be exhausting, I would think. After only a few days, I would have become desperate to arrive at some semblance of permanence. I would want a given landscape to become familiar, where I could become accustomed to specific trees, perhaps, or a reliable source of water. Imagined together, the journey's many challenges suggest that they couldn't reach Canaan soon enough, that God's confirming words in Genesis 12: 6 ("To your offspring I will give *this land*") would be precisely the words they'd waited for: here was home.

But even when they arrive, Abraham doesn't settle. In truth, he never does. In response to God's words in Shechem at the tree of Moreh, he builds an altar—and then moves on, first to a place between Bethel and Ai, and then southward, toward the Negev.

Maybe it was the Canaanites. In 12:6 we learn that the land was full of them. And in 12:10, a famine drives him further south, to Egypt. But even after that disastrous trip, when he has returned again to the tract between Bethel and Ai, Abraham and his people live in tents.

What's more, in a gesture toward settling, he surveys the landscape with Lot and gives him first pick. "Is not the whole land before you? Let's part company. If you go to the left, I'll go to the right; if you go to the right, I'll go to the left," he says. (Genesis 13:9).

In this moment, Abraham sounds as though he's finally going to settle down. If Lot chooses one spot, he'll establish himself in the other, right? But he doesn't do it. Despite the burden of his itinerancy, despite the hope that comes with his promise, Abraham seems implacably resistant to claiming the land that is the seeming answer to all of it.

This is not the case with Lot. Abraham's nephew, by contrast, doggedly seeks to find a home here—with very different results.

• • •

Once upon a time and not very long ago at all, we thought we were going to have to leave home.

In January 2014, I came home to the news from a Bible study, of all things. A Bible study that some friends and I, after careful prayer and planning and study of our own, had put together to help others learn how to study the Bible for themselves.

As if doing such things—in the name of the Lord and of His Word—should protect a person from trouble.

My husband—typically hopeful, mostly joyous—was not with our children in the living room, but stood bracing himself against the kitchen sink, staring out the window into the dark yard.

"We have to sell the house," he said without turning to face me. "We have to sell the house or file for bankruptcy."

"When?" I asked him. In what had amounted to almost thirteen years of varying levels of financial struggle, after becoming practiced in hoping that a deal might come through at the last second, I had become accustomed to asking for—and counting on—time.

"When?" When do we put the house on the market, or file for bankruptcy? How much time to decide which disaster would be ours?

"Tomorrow," he said.

He had lost his job in 2001 but had never spent an idle day. He created a business and then another one; he worked part-time for our church; he ran a music festival for five years. I went back to teaching, and he got a new job in his field that matched his savvy for marketing and his passion for social responsibility—and then the company laid off thousands of people in a single day, my husband among them.

The conversation at the kitchen sink was one of many in which we stared down the precipitous crag of our finances. And all of these conversations were freighted with the spoken and unspoken fears of our inadequacies and of hopes disastrously deferred. But this one rises in my memory as the worst of them all, because the threatened loss—no matter its form— would hit us the next day.

When we went to bed, my husband sat up, elbows on knees, his face in his hands. I had no idea how to encourage him, and neither did I know how to pray. Bankruptcy felt like capitulation, the hard work of those many years lost. But the house, in which we had been raising our children—and our eldest about to graduate from high school—was our home. Selling it would be its own loss, a terrible grief, and a capitulation of its own.

I sat on the bed next to my husband, my arm around his back, my head on his shoulder, and I was already uprooted from it all. We were on a life-raft, not a mattress, and the ocean was wild that night. I pushed my hope toward God: that we were his and that he was ours, come what may. And I wanted desperately to be rescued.

• • •

Lot looked up and saw that the whole plain of the Jordan was well watered, like the garden of the Lord, like the land of Egypt, toward Zoar. (This was before the Lord destroyed Sodom and Gomorrah.) So Lot chose for himself the whole plain of the Jordan and set out toward the east. The two men parted company: Abram lived in the land of Canaan, while Lot lived among the cities of the plain and pitched his tents near Sodom (Genesis 13: 10-12).

Lot wants to be rescued, too. We can have no doubt of it. Remember the travel to the Promised Land, its full 500 miles. Imagine his frustration when, on their arrival in Canaan, his uncle decided *not* to settle down. Recognize that, along with Abraham and his family and all of those possessions—and Lot's too—they had traveled on to Egypt to avoid famine.

No one can blame Lot for his choice. Looking into

that verdancy along the Jordan River, Lot was eager to build a home and to establish the consistency that seems necessary for a flourishing life.

That things don't go well for him after this—and they *don't* go well, things *never* go well for Lot—might have to do with his neighbors and their cultural influence on him and his family. We don't get much in the way of detail on this.

We *do* see him carried off as a spoil of war. A pithy sentence ("They also carried off Abram's nephew Lot and his possessions, since he was living in Sodom" Genesis 14: 12) is the sum of what was surely a life-defining and horrific experience. And later, once established in a house (not a tent) within Sodom's city limits, we witness him offer a saving hospitality to angels of the Lord. But we also see him make a deplorable offer of his daughters to the would-be rapists just outside his door; and we see only him, his wife and daughters saved from raining sulfur that destroys their city.

The latter episode, likely the most notorious of Lot's life, reveals an interesting insistence: the importance of their chosen refuge. Urged by the angels to flee the doomed city and make their way to the mountains, Lot pleads that they be permitted to go to an adjacent town instead.

And warned by the angels to run and *not* look back, Lot's wife nonetheless does so—and is famously turned into a pillar of salt.

I think sometimes, when we are waiting for something, we are like Lot— or his wife. We think we know how things ought to be. We want to stake things out for ourselves, find our comfort, name what is home.

Regardless of the dangers—warring kings, wicked neighbors—Lot was desperate to put down roots. Remember what he saw when he was choosing his home: "the plain of the Jordan... well watered, like the garden of the Lord." No chance of famine here, and the whole expanse haunted by the place we all might like to reclaim: Eden itself.

But Eden is lost to us; home is elsewhere now. Lot's wife looked for it over her shoulder; but Abraham, burdened with the promise, understood it was impossible to find.

• • •

Some families move many times over the course of their lives, over the course of their children's childhoods. It's an adjustment, to be sure, with much hard and practical work on both ends: the packing and unpacking of boxes—not unlike, perhaps, the collapse and then erection of tents. Difficult but do-able. Perhaps nothing to complain about.

My mother moved ten times in the first ten years of her marriage, and one of these moves was to Japan. Herr eleventh move, back to the United States, to Pittsburgh in 1977, was my last until I went to college—and that suited me fine. As a child, I never wanted to move away from Pittsburgh. When I was twelve years old, my parents considered a job opportunity in South Korea, and I threatened to chain myself to our house's water meter.

I wonder if my reasoning was the same as it is now—because I don't want to move now, either. We didn't have to sell our home those few years ago. Unlike so many, we had family step in and give us the financial help we needed. And so we have lived in this house now for nineteen years, and while I imagine that this lack of change has its downsides, and while I feel spoiled for never having had to do the requisite sorting and packing that come with a move, I am very content.

I know that moving would mean adventure—and I like adventure. Moving would also mean adjustment: to new community, church, grocery stores. Difficult, maybe, but not insurmountable. And certainly good for a person.

But there would be much to say goodbye to in moving, and this, for me, is the problem. For starters, there is this house where we raised our children.

Sometimes I try to talk myself out of my attachment to this place. I tell myself that it might mean nothing to leave. A house is just walls, yes? The sun, for example, is the same, shining into your new home. And it's same sun that fell through the rooms of your old house in that familiar way and picked out the motes of dust that held your baby spellbound, reaching, amazed. The same sun whose amber afternoon light lay across the piano and made the wood floor glow in that pattern there. The same that shone through the light of these trees and dappled the entire deck where the children were playing and splashing in the baby pool, the same that shone on the driveway where they stood and waved to the cars as they passed, where they first launched themselves, tentative and thrilled, on their first bicycles with training wheels.

Jesus said, "Do not store up for yourselves treasures on earth, where moth and rust destroy, and where thieves break in and steal. But store up for yourselves treasures in heaven, where moth and rust do not destroy, and where thieves do not break in and steal. For where your treasure is, there your heart will be also" (Matthew 6: 19-21).

It isn't the house that matters, in the end. Neither is it the city, or the fertile valley it rests in. Perhaps Abraham could have told his nephew as much, if Lot had asked.

Do not be afraid, Abraham. I am your shield, your very great reward (Genesis 15: 1).

Which isn't to say that Abraham had all the answers— or that having even some of them meant a life of predictable obedience to God. Abraham's faithfulness is inconsistent at best. His chapters in Genesis can read like a tennis match in which good and evil by turns throttle the ball. First he acts in faith and then he acts in fear and faithlessness, a motif doggedly countered by the favor and mercy of God.

The episodes are more or less familiar: twice Abraham acts in fear for his life, calling his wife his sister and even—to Pharaoh—sending her to live in another man's house. Sarah was apparently very beautiful, and in both cases Abraham believes his being married to her would be a liability, getting him killed so that the Lord of the land could have her.

These are wretched moments: Sarah is a trinket buying Abraham's protection—and this after God has called Himself Abraham's shield.

Then Abraham is Lot's protector. Acting as a general, he rousts the "318 trained men born in his household" and pursues Lot's captors, guiding his men in a formidable military operation to chase those captors down. It's nothing short of a coup: Lot's recovery—and that of his people and possessions—is complete.

This success is followed by a different opportunity to make himself secure: Abraham is basically invited into fellowship with Sodom's king and offered the spoils of war. But Abraham refuses this wealth and would-be protection, recalling again his allegiance to God: "I have raised my hand to the Lord, God Most High, Creator of heaven and earth, and have taken an oath that I will accept nothing belonging to you, not even a thread or the thong of a sandal, so that you will never be able to say, 'I made Abram rich'" (Genesis 14: 22-23). In this moment, his treasure and his hope rest completely in the God of the promise.

But again, his confidence wavers, because God's promise requires a son. Abraham's nation must begin with a child, and at upwards of 75 years old, Sarah is still barren. Despite God's words to Abraham—first in Haran and then displayed in a covenant in Mamre—and despite Abraham's practiced belief in that promise— he and Sarah try to determine things for themselves: through Sarah's maidservant Hagar, Abraham becomes father to Ishmael.

Here is Abraham's effort to make a home: he will pry the awaited promise from God's hand by forcing that hand—and the result is grief. Grief for Sarah, who is mocked by her maidservant. Grief for Abraham, who is subject to Sarah's blame. And grief for Hagar, who flees the only protection she knows to escape an abusive mistress.

Years ago, a friend and I set out to read through Genesis together. We hadn't gotten very far when my friend expressed some unhappiness with the book. She said it was the characters: "Everyone is terrible," she said.

She was right. We have only one true hero in the Bible. Only One who is just, merciful, true and good.

God comes to Hagar's rescue. She doesn't ask for him, but he comes anyway. He directs Hagar to return to the shelter of Abraham's household, and he tells her, "I will so increase your descendants that they will be too numerous to count" (Genesis 16: 10).

• • •

By faith Abraham, when called to go to a place he would later receive as his inheritance, obeyed and went, even though he did not know where he was going. By faith he made his home in the promised land like a stranger in a foreign country; he lived in tents, as did Isaac and Jacob, who were heirs with him of the same promise. For he was looking forward to the city with foundations, whose architect and builder is God (Hebrews 11: 8-10).

I read these words, and I wonder "When?" When was Abraham convinced that he should no longer try to establish a home here? After years of alternatively trusting God and then trying to manage things on his own, when did he finally grasp that he would not in this life "receive the things promised" after all, but should learn to see and "welcome them from a distance"?

We get no "ah-ha" moment, no chapter in which Abraham apparently and fully recognizes that God is faithful and will make good on every word he has spoken. But we see the claim made in Hebrews: that Abraham placed his hope in a city to come, one with foundations that make it sure and lasting, never subject to age or disaster as in so much sulphur raining down from the sky.

And we see that, ultimately, Abraham throws all his hope on the God of the promise, even believing that he can do the impossible—perhaps because with the birth of Isaac, the impossible had already come to pass.

• • •

By faith Abraham, when God tested him, offered Isaac as a sacrifice. He who had received the promises was about to sacrifice his one and only son, even though God had said to him, 'It is through Isaac that your offspring will be reckoned.' Abraham reasoned that God could raise the dead, and figuratively speaking, he did receive Isaac back from death (Hebrews 11: 17-19).

With these words, the writer of Hebrews recalls this defining moment of the Old Testament. In a test of his chosen one's faithfulness, God sends Abraham to Mt Moriah to sacrifice Isaac, the child of the promise.

Because we read these words in Hebrews—that Abraham believed God could raise Isaac from the dead— we might like to imagine that the experience of offering his son in sacrifice wasn't so terrible. And knowing the story's outcome—that God mercifully provided an alternate sacrifice—we can see it all in the safety of retrospect: worst horrors went unrealized.

But I think an honest confrontation of human nature and parental love would tell the story differently. We could imagine it like this:

• • •

Abraham did not sleep during the three-day journey. By day, he fixed his eyes on the mountains ahead. The others' efforts to engage him—Isaac and young Eliezer in their antics, Laban in his respectful solicitations—were soon abandoned. Not long into the first day's walk, they knew the master was deeply troubled; they knew to keep their distance from this one who lagged behind them. Abraham was praying, that much they understood. This was a journey toward sacrifice.

But they didn't know the weight Abraham shouldered, the silence he assumed to protect them and the horror of the task at hand. They couldn't perceive his lips moving; they heard no mumble.The sound that ushered unceasing from his mouth, inaudible to them, was to Abraham's own ear like an echo of the wind: *Yahweh. Yahweh. Yahweh.*

In his despair, he had no other words.

At night, he stood at a distance while the servants set up camp. He accepted none of the food Isaac offered him. He watched the light fade on the mountains and waited with his back to them all until they fell asleep. And when he knew they were sleeping, the rhythms of their breathing set and Laban's snore rising into the darkness, Abraham lay down close to his son.

The stars were bright and cold, innumerable spots of light and also dimly clustered clouds; behind them lay expanses of gauzy light—more stars—and for a moment he wondered where their limits lay, if behind these stars peering down on this desert there weren't more stars lying thickly in multiple, ascending bands. Strata upon strata of stars.

"Look up at the heavens and count the stars—if indeed you can count them. So shall your offspring be."

Yahweh.

• • •

On the second day, eyes fixed on the mountains, Abraham could no longer see them but instead saw the visions playing in his mind, each one a new wound. Here is Isaac just earlier that day, laughing about he knew not what with the young Eliezer, who is only a year or two his senior. These boy-men laughing together, talking endlessly and laughing some more.

And then Isaac, perhaps aged ten, sitting at supper with Abraham and Sarah, now telling them something about his day, tending sheep with Eliezer and Meshech. Abraham can't recall the story Isaac was telling, and this itself is a wound, as is the memory of that gesture Isaac had: pushing his curls off his forehead with a flat palm pressed against his head. He did it all the time, distressing his mother, who thought it was poor manners.

Abraham and Sarah had argued about it, and Isaac, on his own, had abandoned it long ago. Another wound.

When he was very little, Isaac's curls would catch in his father's beard. Before he could talk, just after he learned to move on his own two feet, Isaac would come to where his father sat cross-legged at his tent or under the trees, and he would turn and back into his father's lap, falling into a sitting position with every confidence. His back to his father, his hair tangling in his beard, Isaac offered him whatever he grasped in his plump fist: pebbles, a glittering stone, a chicken feather, a snakeskin, and once, a shower of sand.

Abraham's steps slowed under the weight of this wound. *Yahweh.*

"I will surely bless you and make your descendants as numerous as the stars in the sky and as the sand on the seashore."

Isaac's laughter blew back to him on the desert wind. He was always laughing, this Isaac. The night he told his forgotten story at dinner, the night he again vexed his mother with his flat palm to his head, he had told them something funny and had laughed so hard his milk came out his nose. And this had made him laugh.

he had laughed, too, with Ishmael, in those rare moments that neither boy was with his mother but with their father. Here Abraham saw it: Isaac wasn't walking yet and was sitting in the sand, and Ishmael played with him, hiding behind the shield that Abraham had balanced against the tent's ropes. Abraham sees Ishmael's lean brown legs, the newly curving muscle of his upper arm, his strong brown fingers clutching the edge of the shield.

Abraham groans at the memory, and the sound is carried away from them all, toward Sarah and home.

he sees Ishmael and his mother walking away from him into the desert, Hagar's arms burdened with food and water, the back of Ishmael's bent head. He did not turn around, and Abraham had watched after them until he couldn't see them anymore.

Now he walks with Isaac through the desert. At the foot of the mountain, Abraham instructs Eliezer and Laban to wait. He and Isaac will go up the mountain alone.

"Stay here with the donkey while I and the boy go over there. We will worship and then we will come back to you."

Yahweh. Yahweh. Yahweh.

• • •

Abraham's life is marked by restlessness. Journeys fill and book-end his life. The first is the move out of Ur to Terah, and the last is this test: to Moriah and the mountains, to sacrifice his son.

Surely this is the most terrible moment in the Old Testament: Genesis 22. It all happens fast enough for the reader; we get the full story in nineteen verses. But it can only have been an agony for Abraham, especially in the moments where the narrative slows. For example, we have some conversation, Isaac's only comment, the dreadful question asking the whereabouts of the sacrificial lamb. And his father's answer, full of faith: "God himself will provide the lamb for the burnt offering, my son" (22: 8).

Safely distant from this exchange, the writer in me casts about for a metaphor, some significance in the terrain where Abraham and his son stopped their climb. A level place with plentiful stones to build an altar, where Abraham had perhaps offered sacrifices before. I want it to be a garden, one that echoes Lot's choice of Sodom's valley and recalls the abandoned Eden. Because here is Abraham's home. Here, after years of leaning on God's promise and then wildly veering from it, we watch him put all his hope in God.

I imagine him lifting the stones to build the altar, piling the wood, moving with a pained deliberation that mirrored the agony in his soul, somehow nourishing his faith in the Almighty God who had been gracious to him again and again.

Abraham had had faith when, with Isaac, he left the servants behind at the bottom of the mountain. Knowing the terrible task ahead, he believed in the power of God to restore his son. "*We* will come back to you," he had said.

• • •

The journey down the mountain was a slow one—not because of Abraham this time, but due to Isaac, who moved with heavy steps, like one stunned. He was ashen-faced and silent, his face expressionless.

His father walked next to him, close by. He spoke to him occasionally in a low voice, and when he was not speaking, he was reaching out to his son; clasping his arm, embracing his shoulders, sometimes just holding on to Isaac's sleeve.

The whole way home, Abraham's eyes streamed tears. He wept and wept and only shook his head at the questioning Laban. He had no words yet for what had happened on the mountain.

At night he waited until they were all sleeping, then lay down next to his son. He listened to his steady breathing and then, each night, fell asleep touching him in some way: his hand on his back; on his arm; on the back of his head, his fingers caught in the curls.

He didn't sleep on his back; he didn't see the stars. Instead he slept on his side, his face to Isaac. He saw the low, rumpled line of Isaac's body, and he listened to him breathe.

Yahweh.

• • •

Bill's first job loss back in the summer of 2001 was a small disaster, not uncommon. It was something that millions of others have weathered.

And it was terrifying.

Our wait for consistent income, for the deceptive security of a steady job, would be years.

But I didn't know this on the late summer afternoon when my children were napping and I was folding laundry in the basement. What I knew was the absence of job prospects and a fundamental agony of fear.

With a silent house, busy hands, and an even busier mind, I began again to review how we had arrived here: what were the decisions and steps that landed us in this crisis?

My husband had graduated from one of the top business schools in the world. He had gotten a job and the babies had come along. He had worked hard.

And then he had decided he wanted to try different work, something brand new: an Internet start-up, it was called. A small company with lots of opportunity for growth. Moreover, the company had recently received a significant investment. Promising times, indeed.

Until the money ran out and the job no longer existed. Which was where we were in August 2001, and me and fear folding laundry in the basement.

Unlike some other emotions, fear begs for an answer. It can run towards anxiety or sadness, something bottled and withdrawn. Or it can act out in myriad ways—and here, one of its options is anger.

I was folding bed sheets, and I was considering being angry. Not at the people who had spent all of the investment, but at my husband: for deciding to leave his original job and ply his trade with another—one that eventually ran out.

Folding those sheets, I considered this option for a moment. Anger with my husband seemed worthy and deserved. His decision had landed us in this disaster, hadn't it? Never mind that everyone in his department at his previous job had also lost their jobs and, had he stayed there, he would have been among them. No, I wasn't considering such rational understanding. I was simply terrified and looking for someone to blame.

It was only grace that intercepted these thoughts and showed me—before I understood how none of our circumstances was my husband's fault—that I couldn't possibly blame him. That, were I to do so, I would simultaneously build a wall between us, one that could potentially be far more difficult to surmount than the challenges of income loss and unemployment.

In an instant, I realized I shouldn't blame Bill. I could only trust God. I could choose to receive our frightening and not uncommon problem from His generous hand. I could wait to see what God would do. And I would have to trust Him.

• • •

By faith Abraham, even though he was past age—and Sarah herself was barren—was enabled to become a father because he considered him faithful who had made the promise. And so from this one man, and he as good as dead, came descendants as numerous as stars in the sky and as countless as the sand on the seashore.

All these people were still living by faith when they died. They did not receive the things promised; they only saw them and welcomed them from a distance. And they admitted that they were aliens and strangers on the earth.... They were longing for a better country—a heavenly one. Therefore God is not ashamed to be called their God, for he has prepared a city for them" (Hebrews 11: 11-13, 16a).

I wanted the place for Abraham's sacrifice to function as a metaphor, balancing the Garden lost to Adam and Eve and answering the specious security chosen by Lot. But my metaphor can't rest in any plot of land. And anyway, all of these who were living by faith—Abraham and Sarah and the many other faithful named in Hebrews 11—knew that it wasn't a metaphor or a piece of land they were after. They were looking for an actual city "with foundations, whose architect and builder was God."

Then I realize that of course the metaphor is already present, waiting on the mountain. That terrible day when Abraham, in his obedience, bound his beloved Isaac and raised his knife to kill him, an angel stopped him. God could see that Abraham's faith extended even to the loss of his son. And so Isaac was freed and a ram, its horns caught in some underbrush, was offered in sacrifice.

That ram is the metaphor I'm wanting. It is Abraham and Isaac's rescue, the provision and deliverance they were desperate for, and it is also the pre-figured Lamb of

God, the Son whose death answers the curse that sent us all into exile in the first place.

Abraham descended the mountain together with his beloved Isaac, his heart and mind brimming with the astonishing generosity of God. Home was not the Promised Land, after all. Home was God Himself.

I am your very great reward (Genesis 15: 1).

THREE
EXPECTATION

*I should not love my suffering because it is
useful. I should love it because it is.*

–Simone Weil

A friend shared a story with me, years ago now, about an incident with her two-year-old son. Like many two-year-olds—like many people—he was fond of a snack now and then. I no longer recall what the snack was that day—we'll say it was cookies—but that part doesn't matter. What matters is that this mother (who loved to give good gifts to her children) obliged her little boy and gave him not one, not two, but three cookies. He held one in each hand and had one in his mouth.

What I know I remember correctly is this: she gave him the cookies, and he cried.

He didn't cry because he didn't have what he

needed: as a good mother, she took care of his needs, sometimes before he even knew he had them. Neither did he cry because he didn't have what he wanted (see the aforementioned cookies). No. He cried because he didn't have the bag.

He didn't want to hold two cookies. He wanted to hold *the bag* of cookies. He didn't want to be limited to the generosity–the ample generosity– he could have enjoyed. He wanted to control and be sure of the continued supply.

I am like this. Are you?

• • •

I think we all have expectations. I think we have far more in the way of expectations than we realize. I think expectations precede most of our doings, whether we are flipping a light switch or graduating from college.

Every spring, along with many Bachelor's degrees in the sciences and the arts, the small Christian college my husband and I attended churned out lots of engaged couples.

Those were heady days. After four years in which we students had gradually and increasingly flexed the muscles of our independence, many of us were apparently ready to make the enormous commitment that is marriage. In truth, it seemed like a bigger deal to marry than to simply graduate. With a wedding, one sensed the couple make an irrevocably clean break from home and parents. Where a single adult might take a job in a distant city and move far away—a profoundly independent thing to do—a marriage seemed to signify an even more official rending of the ties to home: if you married, there is no going back.

For those of us marrying or watching friends do so, there was, too, another potential, one signifying to an even greater degree that one had taken the full plunge into adulthood: having children.

To a couple, the question of "when" for children almost always had the same answer: they would wait five years. "We're on the five-year-plan," people would say—and this reply didn't depend on graduate school or a distant move or any immediately pending hurdle.

I think it simply felt safe. Five years was ample time for a couple to learn to live together and to establish themselves in decent jobs. It was maybe even enough time to buy a house.

A part of me looks back on this with cynicism— which is unkind at best, and unfair. A plan is a plan, and having one is wise. The fact that life is bigger than we are and can force those plans to change doesn't alter the discernment of having them in the first place.

And certainly each of us had seen plans go awry. We had watched marriages collapse and jobs disappoint. We had seen failure or joyous surprise require friends and loved ones to renegotiate their lives.

But in the euphoria of newness and our sophomoric

wisdom, we imagined that we ourselves could steer around all that. The problems we had observed for others were ones we would avoid. With confidence, we laid claim to some imagined control: we already had our educations, and now we had found our life's partner. We would get excellent jobs, and our children—coming on time, as predicted, in five years—would be amazing.

And is anything wrong with that? Shouldn't we hope for the best? A positive outlook can make the better half of a big difference much of the time. I think we can all agree on that.

• • •

Long before the words became a book title and some time before I became a mother, my mother used to advise me: "Always have your second baby first." A great if impossible bit of counsel, because for many mothers, anxiety and uncertainty arrive with the baby. Any subsequent births are accompanied by at least some measure of familiarity that helps to make those births and babies, regardless of personality, easier.

Marie was Anna's third baby, so she felt she knew what to expect: the baby would be born early and quickly, and would be over seven pounds. Now Anna admits that these were expectations she didn't realize she had—until those expectations weren't met.

Her first daughter had been a difficult delivery. Two years later, Anna was pleased by how quickly birth of her second daughter had come about. Counseled by her midwife and a delivery nurse, Anna had found that her efforts to help labor along were effective. The seven-hour labor was followed by a mere fifteen minutes of pushing, and the baby was in her arms after only seven and a half hours at the birthing center.

In retrospect, Anna says she should have known the third birth was going differently, as there were marked distinctions even in the middle of the process. But, fixed on her expectation, Anna compared the labors in different ways, accepting suggestions for help based on what had worked for the second birth; doing some things earlier in the process because, last time, they had helped so much.

Still, the labor went far more slowly this time. When encouraged to get some sleep, Anna refused, confident that the baby would be coming soon. And when one midwife finished her shift and the new one arrived, Anna prescribed her expectations to her midwife. "You have an hour," she told her, certain that this labor wouldn't go longer.

In the end, Anna's labor with her third daughter was fifteen hours. The birth was natural; the baby was healthy; there were no lingering complications. But Anna realized she had to get over some disappointment nonetheless. She says, "I had this ideal: I can do *these* things and make *this* happen," but that's not how it turned out.

• • •

Our expectations most definitely get in our way. Which—again— isn't to say that we should anticipate worst-case scenarios. But it is most definitely to say that, when we are waiting on God for his help, action, or deliverance, we should probably try to get past our expectations for how he will act.

No, we shouldn't just try to get past our expectations, we should abandon them. We should absolutely put them down. When we are anticipating the faithful grace and goodness of the living God, we shouldn't try to tell him what that looks like.

See Anna, laboring at the birthing center, unable to fully receive the help offered because she thought she knew how it would go.

Or, if you prefer, observe again my friend's precious two-year-old son. He stands with cookies in good supply, but he can't enjoy them because he had expected the entire bag.

My husband and I may have thought that five years was the right wait for a first baby, but we waited longer than that, wading for a time in the uncertain waters of infertility.

When we name outcomes for God—when we think we know how it should or even how it *will* go—a kind of stubbornness sets in. We grow fond of our expectations because they are so often good, and that fondness strengthens our grip on them. This makes it difficult to be open-handed, to extend our palms to whatever it is he has for us. We're so preoccupied telling him what he *should do* that we are unable to receive and enjoy what he is actually *doing*.

I'm not sure my friend's son ever enjoyed his cookies.

And Anna will tell you, despite her experience and the excellent process, that her labor with Marie was her most difficult—not at all because of the outcome, but because it contradicted and disappointed her expectations.

• • •

Remember what my friend said to me on that long-lost afternoon: "I just want to learn whatever it is I'm supposed to learn from this." And I couldn't blame her. Who wouldn't want to speed this process and so be set free from her wretched discomfort—this suffering— that she was waiting through?

In truth, I can't count how many times I've heard someone say something along those lines. I have said it many times myself. But it struck me anew on that spring afternoon, and I've since realized that the statement belies some unstated assumptions that are likely worth thinking over.

First, we take as given in our waiting that there is something to learn. We are assuming that God is teaching us in whatever we are enduring, and this exposes faith. The bedrock belief here is that our wait is not whimsy, caprice, or unkindness, but rather something that God will make over into fruitfulness. Where this endless waiting feels barren and void of meaning, God will bring new life, significance, even beauty.

This is good.

But what of the other half of the statement, the implied but unspoken "so that...."? "I just want to learn whatever it is I'm supposed to learn from this," we say, leaving off the rest of the sentence because we are in a terrific hurry. What matters here is actually less a "lesson" or result and more perhaps the desire to have it over with. We want to get past this wait, move on from this suffering (and understandably so)— but why? What is it we are wanting? Do we simply want to get back to our normal lives? From the vantage point of this protracted wait, "normal life" sounds spectacular. But if we truly believe that the living God is in the very process of teaching us something, if we understand that the creator of the universe is actively engaged in this wait, then perhaps a "normal life" is not—and never has been—in the cards.

And now we are getting somewhere in terms of understanding our expectations. When we say that we just want to get through—to learn—whatever it is we are supposed to learn, then we are no longer looking expectantly towards the living God, but instead towards an outcome. We want to learn and get past this. We want to check this life-lesson off the list. We want to flip the page on the workbook, get to the next academic level.

We reduce God to a curriculum, one we are working through and one in which we are, at this point, having some significant trouble.

But God is not a curriculum; he is a person. He defines "personhood," which means he is more a person than anyone we've ever known or will know.

• • •

You will recall that our first wait for the security of a steady income began in 2001. At that time, my husband took a part-time job in our new church building as the sound engineer. It wasn't long before Bill and some others saw this larger building as an opportunity to extend the church ministry into our community. And so, over the next few years, Bill pioneered the use of the church auditorium as a concert venue, where a variety of Christian artists came to perform.

Ever the entrepreneur, Bill began to think outside the church-building box. In April 2005, with the vital help of friends and some corporate sponsorships, he held the first Carolina HopeFest at a new venue in downtown Durham. It was a full-scale music festival purposed to raise money for an indigenous non-profit organization in Kenya.

Over the five years of the festival's continuance, we

enjoyed the performances of many nationally known musicians and saw returning visitors from all over the state. Bill began looking into taking the festival abroad—by sea. He was in conversation with Andy Levine of Sixthman, a music cruise company, and he was interested in giving the Carolina HopeFest a cruise opportunity. Meanwhile, by year two of the festival, Bill had gotten a full-time job for an international company, where he served as the director of corporate social responsibility.

And then came that other event that I've already mentioned, that day in January of 2009, when Bill and several thousand others at his company very suddenly lost their jobs.

We were stunned. We had just begun to feel we were getting back on our feet. We had (mostly) trusted God throughout the terrors and disappointments the first time, then here came round two.

Some psychologists credits job loss as one of the biggest stressors of modern life. Some compare its strain with that of losing a loved one. And while at this point I had a teaching job which provided a small but steady income, the loss was a blow—practically, psychologically, and even spiritually. Why would God let this happen again?

A small but significant side-effect was that the HopeFest would have to be suspended. Suddenly scrambling to reinvent himself professionally, Bill couldn't give personal time to the project. Among others who loved the Festival, Levine knew we wouldn't be able to send the HopeFest on a cruise, but he still (very kindly) wanted to give us a taste of the experience.

And so it was that, a few months after losing his job, my husband and I were given free tickets for a weeklong Caribbean music cruise that included the talents of Lyle Lovett, the Indigo Girls, and Shawn Colvin.

Here is the reason I've told you all this: One afternoon on the cruise, Bill went for a jog around the top deck of the ship. Among other things, this deck held a running track and a play area for young children.

As he made his circuit around the track, Bill passed a young family. Two very young children, two parents, and a young woman who looked to be the children's nanny. Bill passed them once. He passed them again. And he found himself becoming annoyed. No, not annoyed. Bill was angry.

He told God what he thought, which went something like this: Who is this guy, who can afford to take his wife, two kids and a *nanny* on this cruise? Do they have two separate cabins? Two staterooms? What is it like to have a job that enables you to do something like that? And what makes this guy better than me? Is he smarter than I am? More employable? Why can't *I* do what he's doing?

So he thought, and so he ran, all the while angry at God for what had been given to this family, and what had *not* been given to him.

Until Bill realized—his thoughts intercepted by divine kindness and a searing conviction—that he most certainly *had* been given this. He had been given it at *no expense to himself.* All of it was a gift, and if he lacked proof, he needed to note that he was jogging around the upper deck of a cruise ship in the Caribbean, afloat with his wife on a music cruise that he hadn't paid for but (until the jealousy-ridden jog) was thoroughly enjoying.

Bill's expectation was not that he wouldn't get to do some nice things in his lifetime, but rather that he would pay for these things out of his own pocket. He would achieve, and he would succeed, and marks of that success would look like Caribbean cruises or a fancy house, maybe. He would make amazing things happen.

That day he was staring a gift in the face, surrounded by the beauties of the blue-green sea, but he couldn't see it clearly because his expectations clouded his vision.

He had a cookie in each hand.

Yes, expectations can provide structure and vision for our lives, but they can be downright dangerous when we're waiting on God.

The Israelites, released by miracle and laden with Egyptian wealth, teach us this in the desert.

Or do they? How many of us, reading their story, tend to shake our heads, wondering how in the world they could be so faithless? They certainly don't teach by example.

"Israelites!" (We want to shout to them, having clambered onto some desert rock outcropping worthy of Charlton Heston.) "Israelites!" (We know we have to say it at least twice; they are so numerous and spread out before us on the shores of the Red Sea.) "How can you possibly be doubting God now? Have you lost your minds? Were the ten plagues not enough?"

But we all know the story. The Israelites are heedless—to us, to Moses. To anyone. And also it's very difficult to make ourselves heard over the thundering horde of chariots that is headed their way.

They heard the horde before they saw it. It probably sounded like distant thunder—and everyone had had enough of thunder during the curse of the hail. They didn't know what they were hearing and didn't imagine it to be Pharoah. Exodus tells us that the Israelites "were marching out boldly"(Exodus 14:8) at the time. In those incipient hours or even days of their freedom, the Israelites were incredulous, overjoyed, bold—and definitely not anticipating that Pharaoh would be headed their way.

And then the dust clouds appeared, ballooning along the horizon because Pharaoh brought out no less than "six hundred of the best chariots, along with all the other chariots of Egypt, with officers over all of them" (14:6). Likely it was very little time before the Israelites realized what was almost upon them, and it was terrifying to comprehend the size of the pursuing army.

Pharaoh had brought everyone available: all his "horses and chariots, horsemen and troops" (14:9). The entire military enterprise was running the Israelites down.

Which is why the Israelites—were they able to hear us crying out to them from our desert rock—would pay no attention to us at all. In front of them is the Red Sea, and behind them is Pharaoh and the Egyptian army.

For the purposes of our conversation, one might say that their expectations were incredibly low: death was certain and imminent.

Here are their cries to the Lord, their cries to Moses: "'Was it because there were no graves in Egypt that you brought us to the desert to die? What have you done to us by bringing us out of Egypt? Didn't we say to you in Egypt, 'Leave us alone; let us serve the Egyptians?'" (14:11-12).

Despite the miraculous plagues they had witnessed in Egypt—ten of them; despite God sparing them in Goshen from seven of those ten plagues; despite the fearsome deliverance they had received through obedience in preparing the Passover Lamb—the Israelites lost all hope.

This is not because of what they *had* seen. They had already seen God keep his word. "I will be with you" (Exodus 3:12), he had said to Moses, and then they were led by a pillar of cloud by day and a pillar of fire at night. "You will plunder the Egyptians" (3:22), he had said. At that very moment, the Israelite children trembled in fear in their Egyptian silver and gold: they were wearing fine Egyptian clothes.

But now it would seem the Israelites are blind to these gifts, because their vision is clouded by dust and their ears are filled with thunder. Instead they cling to despair and the misery of their enslavement: "'It would have been better for us to serve the Egyptians than to die in the desert!' they cried" (14:12).

I wonder if any of them heard Moses's answer above the din: "'Do not be afraid. Stand firm and you will see the deliverance the Lord will bring you today. The Egyptians you see today you will never see again. The Lord will fight for you; you need only to be still" (14:13-14).

Moses offers them an exchange: they should trade their doomsday expectations for belief in the living God. And then God works a miracle on their behalf. Again.

The book of Exodus appropriately erupts in the Israelites' song of praise after this, a song that continues for eighteen verses. And even after this, Moses's sister Miriam leads the women of Israel in continued singing and dance. The fact is that God's deliverance of his people here is absolutely stunning. I seriously doubt any one of us could have scripted it.

• • •

Our expectations of God, rooted in what we think we want or born in a cradle of need, cannot take into compass the extent of his power and vision. This doesn't mean that we shouldn't tell him these expectations. It absolutely doesn't mean that we should give up asking for what we think we need or want. In his Sermon on the Mount, Jesus commands us to ask, reminding us that our Father knows what we need before we even ask him (Matthew 6:32). And he goes on to tell us that, in response to our requests, he will "give good gifts to those who ask him" (7:1).

The problem is never that we need something; it is never that we bring him our desire. The problem is in telling him how he ought to answer it.

• • •

The disciples, seasoned over three years of traveling with Jesus, listening to him teach, seeing him heal people, watching him answer combative Pharisees, believed him to be the Son of God. Even after Christ's divisive words about eating his flesh and drinking his blood—references to his physical death as atonement for sin—the Twelve remained with him.

"You don't want to leave, do you?" Jesus asked them.

And Peter's faith-filled answer: "Lord, to whom shall we go? You have the words of eternal life. We believe and know that you are the Holy One of God" (John 6:67-69).

But even these disciples misunderstood him, their expectations of the Messiah decidedly informed by what they thought it meant to be God's chosen people, and also by the challenges and injustice of the Roman occupation. They were with him when he rode into Jerusalem cheered by a large crowd, many of whom had traveled there for the Passover.

This crowd was effectively naming him king. The palm branches they waved were signs of victory, and their words claimed him as their rescue and deliverance.

And yet Jesus was riding on a donkey, which an acceptable ride for a prince. But I think they missed its second, essential significance: in entering Jerusalem this way, Jesus identified himself as a king who came in peace. Despite the expectation of the crowd, the Son of God was not coming to overthrow Roman rule and re-establish Israel as a sovereign nation.

You might think the disciples would understand differently. Jesus had predicted his death to them numerous times. He does so again, just after this celebratory march into the city.

But like the hopes of those waving palm branches, the disciples' hopes are informed by their expectations, and they are unable to read the signs. John simply tells us that they didn't understand (12:16).

We see this even in their last moments together. Jesus has washed the disciples' feet; they have eaten supper together. He has sent out his betrayer, and the rest of them have walked with him to the Mount of Olives for prayer.

When Judas, some soldiers, and temple officials

arrive to arrest Jesus, Peter still believes in immediate triumph. In a shocking act of violence, he pulls out his sword and cuts off the ear of a high priest's servant.

I wonder if all of them carried weapons, if other disciples, emboldened by the brash Peter, also suddenly brandished swords. Maybe they believed this was the start of it, that they would kill this band of soldiers and, led by the Messiah Jesus, march together into Jerusalem.

Other followers would join them as they went. The crowd who just the day before had sung Jesus' praises would flood once again into the streets. Armed with their own weapons and the miraculous powers of the Christ, they would rush into the center of the city. They would storm the palace and rout the soldiers. They would overthrow Pilate, Herod, and anyone else in their path.

But, "Enough of this!" (Luke 22: 51) Jesus says, and immediately they are quiet.

He bends and picks up the torn and piteous ear, ignoring the blood that covers his hands. He makes his way to the injured servant who stands apart, bending away from them all into the grove of olive trees, clutching a curved palm over the side of his bleeding head.

Jesus grasps him by the shoulder, gently turns him around, and with his bloodied hand sets the ear in place. The bleeding stops, the pain is gone.

Then Jesus turns back to the gaping mob of soldiers

and disciples. They stand silent, waiting. He asks them what, exactly, they were expecting.

"Did you think I was leading a rebellion?" (22: 52), he says.

Their answer is yes. Some wanted to follow him into that rebellion, others were there to stop it.

But Jesus was doing something completely different.

• • •

She was almost 28 years old in 1974 when her first baby was born. She and her husband had already been married seven years, and her husband was now 37. Her only sibling, who had married two years before her, was already mother to three children. Now Annie had a long-hoped-for baby boy.

When the baby was about three months old, she discovered a lump in her neck, just to the left of her Adam's apple. Soon it was giving her discomfort when she swallowed. She imagined it sitting close to or even on her vocal cords, and her first fear was that she would lose her ability to sing to her baby.

She was afraid of lots of things, of course, cancer chief among them. Cancer in her neck could mean that it also lurked elsewhere in her body. And here she was with a newborn. She knew she needed to see a doctor, but she was terrified by the potential diagnosis.

One day, as she prayed about it with a friend, Annie was given a vision: Jesus stood before her, holding something out to her on a tray. Somehow—in the way of dreams—she knew that whatever was on the tray was what was in her neck.

In the vision, Jesus spoke to her: "Will you look at what I have for you?" he said.

Annie couldn't look. She was sure that the tray held cancer, and looking at it would only confirm that fear. Yet still he waited in the vision, patiently holding the tray. "Look," he said. "Just look."

Annie can't recall how long the vision lasted or how long she resisted that gentle invitation. But when she finally did look, she saw that the object on the tray was his heart.

I realize that this seems an odd story. First of all, questions might arise as to what a heart on a tray might look like, how a vision of that sort could be peace-filled rather than revolting. Then perhaps there are questions about having visions at all. Maybe mystical experiences and prayers for healing have never been part of your relationship with God. That's fine, of course. The miraculous can be discerned in all manner of ways.

But this vision really did come to my aunt during a prayer for healing when my cousin was only a few months old. She had expected that cancer in all its deformed ugliness would be sitting on that tray. She really did think that she would be diagnosed with cancer.

In the midst of that prayer, when Annie saw a vision

of Christ holding out his heart, her fear disappeared completely. Not long after that, also during a time of prayer and before she went to a doctor, the lump in her neck disappeared, too.

I've heard my aunt tell this story numerous times. I've asked her to repeat it to me, fascinated and moved by it, wanting to be sure I've heard it right. I find it far easier to tell than another story I love, a story two thousand years older, far better known and profoundly more mysterious.

I've tried, but I don't know how to adequately imagine the chill in the air, the damp at the feet, or—before these—the cold sadness in her soul that roused Mary from her bed and sent her to the tomb that morning. My guess is that she hadn't slept that night and hadn't slept the night before either, the night they took his body down.

She had helped to wrap him, a body familiar in its way but now so marred by abuse that it might have been anyone. I don't know how to articulate for Mary—or to imagine for myself—the staggering sense of loss and hopelessness.

Yet I know that both of these were Mary's understanding. Her Lord was already lost to her when she made her way to the tomb. Finding it gaping and empty, Mary could only comprehend further loss. She went back to town and said to Peter and John, "They have taken the Lord out of the tomb, and we don't know where they have put him!" (John 20: 2).

Did she speak with these disciples when, breathless, she reached them again? They had run ahead of her to the tomb. John had stared into it from the entrance; Peter had gone inside. We know from the Gospel that John believed, but what of Peter? Did the three of them discuss the possibilities in that waking garden as the light began to rise?

Again, I don't know how to imagine it, but Mary's sense of loss runs so deep that she is unmoved by John's hope, if he shared it with her. And she is unmoved by the sight of and conversation with two angels seated inside the tomb, marking the place where Jesus lay.

She even repeats herself to them, almost the same words she had said to the disciples. Her Lord is gone. His body has been taken, and now she cannot have even the ritual of grief—caring for his body—that was to be her remaining act of love (20:13).

She is so certain he is dead that she doesn't recognize him when he speaks to her—until, of course, he says her name.

Maybe someday I will better be able to imagine that story. Maybe someday—and I fear it—I will know loss in such a way that I will better be able to comprehend Mary's eventual joy. Because *that* part of the story—the moment when she hears his voice speaking her name, calling her irrevocably out of all the deepest sadness—is the part I only *merely* imagine.

I do think, however, that Mary and my aunt would tell you a similar thing of their experiences. What for Mary was the real body of her risen Lord briefly clasped in her arms was for my aunt only a vision, but Annie articulates it well enough. She tells me what Christ was saying to her: "I will never give you anything more than myself."

Neither could we ask for anything more than that. What more could there possibly be?

FOUR
EXPECTANCY

*After the amazing delight and liberty of realizing
what Jesus Christ does, comes the impenetrable
darkness of realizing who he is.*

–Oswald Chambers, *My Utmost For His Highest*

To be told that one shouldn't expect what one wants or needs is rough. After all, beginning at our birth this world is basically the limit of our view, in all its beauties and shortcomings. How to disengage ourselves from expectation—from naming what it is we obviously (so it seems) need and direct our gaze elsewhere, especially (as I prescribe here) on One we haven't seen?

We don't have Mary's advantage, that tear- and joy-filled embrace near the tomb, firm proof under our palms of the physical body of the risen Christ. And yet here should be all our hope.

In the years immediately after Bill lost his job the first time, we experienced many occasions when the money we had simply wasn't enough. I knew I was supposed to trust in God, but what I wanted was cash. I remember being alone of an afternoon in the living room, all the children napping, perhaps, or out playing with friends, and I was praying and crying, desperate that God should help us. I shook my fist at the ceiling, staring upward as if I could see him, knowing that he would care for us in some vague and biblical and potentially impractical way, and saying through clenched teeth: "We live *here.*"

Meaning, of course, that the promises of his blessing were all well and good, but our situation demanded practical assistance, and soon.

Later, I recalled a similar scene in Frank Capra's *It's a Wonderful Life*. This is after a despondent George Bailey leaps into a river to rescue an apparent attempted suicide. The ensuing conversation between him and the man he rescued reveals that the man is Clarence Oddbody, an angel who is actively seeking to rescue George from despair.

Bailey isn't grateful to have an angel looking after him. In truth, this detail barely seems to register. He is bitter over his need and tells Clarence in no uncertain terms that the help he requires is money. With a glimmer of hope, he asks Clarence if he *has* any money, to which Clarence replies that he does not.

"Where I come from, we don't need money," he

explains.

George Bailey's response: "Well, it comes in pretty handy down here, bub."

That's what I wanted to say to God. That is, in fact, what I said to God on more than one occasion. I had heard all my life about his peace, his joy, his abundant life, but I wanted a bank account in the black.

• • •

I realize I was not alone in this—that I am not alone in thinking this way. When we are waiting, we all tend to fix our gaze on what we are waiting for.

The gift—and the difficulty—come in the realization that we all long infor more than what we're waiting for, tha hit the promises of God go somehow beyond that thing we wish to hold in our proverbial hands.

Mary, grasping her resurrected savior, had to let him go. "Do not hold on to me," Jesus said, "for I have not yet returned to the Father" (John 20:17). He was raised from the dead, and Mary had what she thought she wanted, but Jesus had more to do. There was yet more joy to come.

• • •

So how is it done? How do we lift our gaze above that thing we are waiting for? What does that look like?

For insight, I offer you Sylvia Plath's poem "Black Rook in Rainy Weather." Here our poet seems to have given up finding hope—for inspiration, perhaps; for insight; for a sense of divine presence—in the material world. We might take a note or two from this.

See the many ways she describes life around her. The weather is "desultory," the leaves, falling in the rain, do so "without ceremony, or portent." Standard objects, such as kitchen furniture, are "obtuse," and the landscape itself is "dull, ruinous." Her world is firm and material, and it is also mute.

She isn't complaining: "I do not expect a miracle/ Or an accident/to set the sight on fire/in my eye," she says. She no longer expects the world around her to produce flashes of insight, despite the fact that she has seen insignificance suddenly transformed. "A celestial burning," or an angel that "may choose to flare suddenly" at her elbow has imbued a thing or moment with meaning.

But these experiences seem to be firmly in the past, and she is resolved to live without them: she will "patch together a content of sorts." We don't understand what exactly she longs to receive, what she means by a revelation that eases her "fear of total neutrality." She might be speaking of God or faith, or even of the life of a poet, one that might thrive on finding meaning where everything seems otherwise empty.

What I love is that, here in these stanzas, she ultimately affirms a kind of vigil. She says, "I now walk wary...skeptical, yet politic," because "miracles occur."

She isn't demanding a given response from the world or God, but she remains aware of possibility. "The wait's begun again," she says—whatever the "miracle" might be, and whatever it might mean this time.

Hers is a posture of expectancy.

• • •

Like expectation, expectancy is hopeful, but it is less fixed. It doesn't name its outcome, and for that reason it is far more liberating.

My husband and I dated for ten months and were engaged for ten more before we married. I distinctly remember a conversation we had during that time; in fact, I wrote it down. We had been imagining how our lives might go, and for some reason, I recall the possibility of earning pilot's licenses.

Wouldn't that be exciting, we thought? Then we could rent a little plane and get ourselves wherever we wanted to go! Or maybe we would be wealthy enough to own one!

It didn't feel completely out of reach: I think one of his family friends had their own plane. Why not us?

I was excited by this, of course—this and other potentials. Our life together was going to be wonderful, and we were just on the cusp of its beginning. I could imagine so much, all of it new and exciting. I said, "So many great things might happen!"

And Bill replied, "Yes, and the most wonderful of all

is what *will* happen."

With the optimism of the newly graduated, we never imagined financial issues becoming a strain. We weren't utter fools, but we certainly believed ourselves capable—as I said in an earlier chapter—of steering around the difficulties that hobbled the lives of others. Undoubtedly an assumption like that is laced with ignorance, and also some pride. We have long since repented.

But I don't for a moment question the faith underneath Bill's statement. We understood that we would know the goodness of God beyond our hopes for a life in this world.

We really did believe it.

• • •

Sovereign Lord, as you have promised, you now dismiss your servant in peace. For my eyes have seen your salvation, which you have prepared in the sight of all people, A light of revelation to the Gentiles and for glory to your people Israel (Luke 2: 29-32).

As we have already seen, despite the many times he told them, Jesus's disciples don't fully comprehend who he is until after his resurrection. They are the closest to him, the ones he lives with, talks to, spends time with. And still their belief is limited, stunted by their expectations.

His family, too—despite prophecy and the visitation

of angels—doesn't seem to understand. His own mother, whose life he dramatically interrupted with a very surprising pregnancy, nonetheless expresses astonishment when, at twelve years old, Jesus declares that Jerusalem's temple is his Father's house (Luke 2:49).

For the most part, the Pharisees never see him clearly. They, too, are snagged on expectations such as where the Messiah ought to come from and, I think it fair to say, raging jealousy.

Even John the Baptist has his moment of doubt (Matthew 11:3).

Only two I can think of come to him in unmitigated belief: Simeon and Anna, at the temple in Jerusalem when Jesus was eight days old.

The story comes to us in only a few verses in Luke's gospel. In obedience to the law (Exodus 13:2), Mary and Joseph take their baby to the temple in Jerusalem to present him to God. Both Simeon and Anna—perhaps strangers to each other but most certainly strangers to this family—recognize the infant Jesus as the long-awaited Messiah.

Rembrandt might have been fascinated by these two. In oil, etching, and drawing (the latter a study for an eventual painting), he represented them separately or together eight different times. The earliest rendering dates 1628, and others are scattered through his career. His *Simeon's Song of Praise*, 1669, found unfinished at the back of his studio, is credited as the last oil painting of his life.

Some of the artist's interest might have stemmed from the age of his subjects. Apparently artists in Rembrandt's time often painted elderly faces in an effort to build their reputations; perhaps effective renderings of the marks of age was highly valued, and certainly Simeon and Anna were elderly. According to Luke's gospel, the Holy Spirit told Simeon he would live to see the Messiah, and on seeing and holding Jesus, Simeon claimed God's kept promise and said he could die in peace. Anna's age is given. After seven years of marriage, she lived until she was 84. We don't know how old she was the day that Mary and Joseph carried their baby boy into the temple, but Luke calls her "very old" (Luke 2:36).

So Simeon and Anna are perfect candidates for Rembrandt's focus on the elderly. He was a master of the portrait; perhaps he liked bringing his vision of them to life. And their lives were extraordinary if quiet. Simeon was known for his devotion to God and righteousness, and Anna lived out her days worshipping in the temple, fasting and praying. Their faces would have worn lines and creases of age and of hope amidst suffering.

I like to think there is another reason. Rembrandt made masterful use of chiaroscuro, a painting technique employing light to powerful effect. In his paintings, light emphasizes facial features, explores character, and in grander tableaux evokes revelation and emotional power. In his paintings of Simeon and Anna, light floods and shadows their faces, and in those representations including the Christ-child, light seems to come from the baby himself and bathes the figures around him, most powerfully these two who recognize his being the Messiah even in his infancy.

Of course I can't claim that Rembrandt was drawn to the pair's expectancy, but I find his return to them interesting. It might be fair to assert that he appreciated the power of those brief moments, when an impoverished pair from Galilee entered the temple with a newborn son and two pigeons, the latter a purification sacrifice.

How could Simeon and Anna know that here was the Messiah? They were each given revelation, but it was the same offered to all of Israel: out of his own people, God would bring salvation. The prophecy cioursed through the scriptures; it was studied by priests and scholars and discussed in the synagogues and temple.

I think the difference lies in a posture of expectancy. Unlike the Pharisees, who seemed bent on building their reputations through certitude, there's nothing about Simeon or Anna that suggests posturing. From what Luke has to say, each of them seems fixed not on what God will give to them—and to Israel and the world—but on God himself. Thus Simeon was able to hear the Holy Spirit's promise that he would live to see the Christ, and he was responsive to the Holy Spirit's prompting—which is what sent him to the temple courts that day.

And Anna spent her days and nights in worship, which at bottom is nothing more than the humble recognition of who one is and, by contrast, the awed praise of God.

This is not to say that they weren't looking for something from God: they were. They were looking and waiting for what he had promised, "the consolation of Israel." It's just that they didn't decide what that consolation would look like, and so they were able to recognize him when he came.

• • •

To wait in expectancy rather than expectation requires humility. It acknowledges one's limitations, both in power and perspective, and trusts in the limitless power and goodness of God.

It is also an exercise and a practice, a decision that sometimes contradicts everything that seems natural and right. Which is why it is also essential to root it, again and again, in the Word of God. There we find his promises and also myriad revelations of his character, and it's on these things we must pin our hope.

• • •

I was young and now I am old, yet I have never seen the righteous forsaken or their children begging bread (Psalm 37:25).

To be honest, I am not sure how to read verses like this. It seems dangerous to me, calling down all kinds of potential judgment on people who are destitute, as if their poverty is an affliction stemming from moral failure.

Moral failure can certainly lead to destitution, but one can get there by other means, believe me. And does this verse mean, by extension, that those who are truly righteous might never come upon desperate times, might never—in the history of the world—starve to death?

I think this verse is to be taken in concert with the full Psalm, which is about the deceit of wickedness and the faithfulness of God. The life of the wicked might look good, the psalmist says. Their lives might seem enviable due to their wealth. But material wealth is actually immaterial; it is fleeting and empty. By comparison, the righteous might actually own little— but their inheritance is in none other than God himself.

Throughout, the psalmist directs the reader's gaze to God. "The salvation of the righteous comes from the Lord; he is their stronghold in time of trouble. The Lord helps them and delivers them; he delivers them from the wicked and saves them, because they take refuge in him" (Psalm 37:39-40).

In my experience, scripture is pretty relentless on this score. The living God is real, powerful, gracious, holy, and merciful, and all hope rests in him. And while scripture uses specific language and precise images, we're helped to understand that, in some contexts, scripture is poetry making use of metaphor.

In truth, all provision spoken of in scripture is a metaphor, because all provision is Christ. And because Christ was provided for us, we can trust him for provision in the lesser things. As Paul says, "he who did not spare his own Son, but gave him up for us all—how will he not also, along with him, graciously give us all things?" (Romans 8:32).

• • •

To you, O Lord, I lift up my soul;
In you I trust, O my God.
Do not let me be put to shame,
Nor let my enemies triumph over me (Psalm 25: 1-2).

So, fast-forward (again) to 2014, and our family is on the brink of bankruptcy. We are also about to see our firstborn graduate from high school, and as this story of financial struggle began shortly after the birth of our third child, we are powerfully aware of how long we've been waiting and how weary we are.

Understand that every year between 2001 and 2014 was not a desperate one. My husband had some steady employment for a time in there, as did I. But in the balance of years, the scales were tipped in favor of those without a steady income; and debt, combined with the inconsistent income of my husband's new business in real estate, made the first months of 2014 ugly.

Add to this a second demon, one that haunts us all

in various ways: fear of judgment. Unlike some other forms of loss or suffering, financial issues often seem traceable to some failing on the part of the one suffering. You lost your job? Well, what did you do wrong? You lost *another* job? That's *definitely* on you.

No one actually said this to us. And we were surrounded and encouraged by loving friends and family. But the demons of judgment don't have to be audible for us to hear them: in this regard, as in so many others, we are our own worst enemy.

For me, the potential of bankruptcy fit into a judge-worthy category. It was one thing to pinch and scrape, to go into debt and barely squeak by. It was another— and it seemed to feel like another to my husband— to surrender to loss and call it quits, to have our debt erased and also, for a time, our credit destroyed.

Famous and successful people have rather famously filed for bankruptcy. Abraham Lincoln is one, as are Walt Disney and Henry Ford. Filing for bankruptcy is not the end of the world. It may many times be the better part of wisdom.

But in January of 2014, bankruptcy felt like the hopeless end of the line, like the very thing we had tried and prayed so hard to avoid all those years. It felt like shame.

I remembered feeling a thin hope when finding a Bible verse that seemed to answer this concern: "No one whose hope is in you will ever be put to shame, but they will be put to shame who are treacherous without excuse" (Psalm 25:3). Here was a verse I could stake a claim to, I thought. My husband hoped in God, as did I. And here was God's very word, telling us that this hope would spare us.

I mentioned this to my pastor's wife, not so much seeking her opinion as I was telling my friend of my relief. We were standing in a buffet line at church, the weekly community dinner. Who knows how I phrased it to her as I spooned pasta onto my plate? Maybe I was matter-of-fact: "See? We *can't* go bankrupt!" or maybe I was more cautious, aware of my potential misinterpretation.

No matter how I said it, I can affirm that Rebecca's response was two things: gentle and honest. She pointed out that our avoidance of shame has never been God's priority. Think of the prophets, she said, and Ezekiel came to mind, lying on his left side for 390 days and on his right for 40, all in obedience to God and in an effort to call God's chosen people back to himself.

Or of Christ, who scorned the shame of the cross— meaning he decided not to care about the shame but endured it anyway—in order to buy my life.

And then she pointed out that the shame we will avoid when our hope is in him is none other than the shame of sin. When we trust in him, she said, he is faithful to keep us, and we will never be put to shame in his eyes.

That's the shame the verse was talking about. That's the shame that matters.

Oh. Right.

• • •

In 538 B.C., Cyrus of Persia ruled over an empire stretching from northern Africa to the Indus River. His army had subsumed that of the Babylonians and, with it, taken into its cities vast numbers of exiled Jews whose homeland lay along the eastern edge of the Mediterranean Sea.

For the Jews, identity resided strongly in that territory, the Promised Land God had first given to their forefather Abraham. And in 538, Cyrus decreed that the Jews be allowed to return to Jerusalem and rebuild their destroyed temple.

The prophet Haggai records his exhortations to these returned Jews. God has called them to rebuild the temple, and Haggai reminds them of the blessings of obedience. I think the people must have been filled with expectation. They had a specific task to do, and some of them remembered the former temple, built by Solomon. Perhaps they imagined a structure of equal or greater significance, and they looked toward a day when they would no longer be ruled by foreign empires.

The Lord spoke to them through his prophet: "I will shake all nations, and the desired of all nations will come, and I will fill this house with glory" (Haggai 2:7).

These words might have affirmed those expectations. God would "shake all nations," meaning that foreign empires would be overthrown. And while the "desired" could mean treasure, it could also refer to an individual, in which case it signifies the same consolation of Israel awaited by Simeon and Anna, the Messiah himself. In any case, the Hebrews hearing these words would have been filled with tremendous hope in the coming restoration of their temple, the beauty and power of a nation obedient to God.

But God reminds his people that their expectations for this temple and its treasures are inadequate: "'The silver is mine and the gold is mine,' declares the Lord Almighty. 'The glory of this present house will be greater than the glory of the former house,' says the Lord Almighty. 'And in this place I will grant peace,' declares the Lord Almighty" (Haggai 2:9).

The problem with our expectations, as I have said, is that they are never adequate. They tie us down; they bind us to the very limited and fleeting comforts of this world.

When, by contrast, we look to God with expectancy, he fills our lives with hope. "No eye has seen, no ear has heard, and no mind has conceived the things God has prepared for those who love him" (1 Cor. 2:9). I think this passage from Haggai echoes the inconceivability of God's good plan. See, in the passage above, the prophet's use of repetition. As prophet of the Lord, he *should* be speaking the words God has for him. That's what we expect. Yet his phrasing there in verse nine is striking: he tells us three times that this is God speaking. It's as if the news is too good to be true, as if Haggai himself is overwhelmed by the vision God casts here. "I'm not saying this," he seems to say. "This comes from the Lord Almighty."

It's as if Haggai can't get his message across clearly enough. There aren't comprehensible words for us to understand or imagine what the promised glory will look like, so we have to consider the source.

• • •

Fast-forward now to late November, 2016, the day after Thanksgiving.

It's morning and our children—two near-adults and one full-grown—are still asleep. My husband and I sit content in the living room, sipping coffee and watching sunlight move through the golden leaves outside. In our part of North Carolina, some trees still have leaves at Thanksgiving.

Our oldest son is over a year returned from his gap year travels, where he served with Mercy Ships in Madagascar. There he met a young woman from British Columbia, and they are engaged to be married in July of the following year. Our middle son, nearly eighteen, is in his senior year of high school; and our daughter, fifteen, is a sophomore. Each of them is a delight to us and our community, and each of them loves Jesus.

Bill and I are chatting with gratitude about these things: our marriage, our children, our church, his growing business, the book I just released two months before. For a moment, we look at the years that have accumulated behind us.

"How were we so happy then?" Bill says, and I know what he means. He is talking about those lean years, some of which we lived below the poverty line. "How were we so happy?"

And then he lists for me some blessings he sees, the gifts that it seems were imparted to us *because* we didn't have money: how it was a gift to our children that we couldn't give them everything, that maybe the mild privation helped shape who they've become.

Or maybe, ourselves streamlined because we couldn't set our hope on the material accumulations of this life, we were able to teach them or simply show by example what it looks like to throw all our hope on God.

We can't know, and neither do we like to assume we do. We don't know what lies ahead, what challenges will yet come to our faith or that of our children. But we've begun to learn a hope that means living in expectancy: that God is good, that we will see his goodness in whatever way he chooses to show it to us. That whatever way he chooses is the very best way.

• • •

Moses learned this, too.

Let's remember that he hadn't wanted to do it. Living happily in Midian, Moses liked his life as a shepherd. The quiet and anonymity suited him.

But God chose him to lead his people out of Egypt. He chose him to confront Pharaoh and work miracles along the Nile. He chose him to explain to the Israelites the extraordinary deliverance: sacrificed lambs and blood on doorposts.

At first things looked good. The initial departure was confident, and the triumph at the Red Sea absolute. There was the near-chapterfull of praise, the women singing and dancing their hearts out to God. And there were the pillars of cloud and fire, the manna and the quail, water gushing from a rock.

Moses grasped God's vision, the one he cast for his servant on Sinai: a tabernacle, the ark of the covenant, the covenant itself. God would dwell among them; there was law to show them how to live; and out there, beyond the horizon, was a Promised Land.

But there was complaining, too, the periodic choir of misery, so much in the way of accusations and whining. The nature of this people became more and more apparent as the months and years wore on. Moses called them stiff-necked and certainly meant nothing flattering by it. He went to God on their behalf, but he also griped to God about them. And of course God saw it for himself, a final straw of sorts coming at the very edge of the Promised Land, when ten out of twelve spies declared the land unconquerable. This lack of faith was rewarded with forty more years of wandering before they were finally home.

Here was one among many moments when Moses confronted the reality of his task. The thrill and drama of their initial exodus from Egypt, the splash and surprise of their triumph at the Red Sea were not the stuff of everyday. No, this move to the Promised Land was a slow burn. Moses has an endurance game that goes beyond most—if not all—of the famous figures of the Old Testament.

And at the end of Deuteronomy, the nation he has led stands again at the edge of the Promised Land. After all of those years of struggle and suffering, Moses knows he won't be going in: Joshua will lead them home.

But we get no words of complaint from him, perhaps because somewhere in the desert over those long and dry years, Moses shifted his gaze from expectation to expectancy. He long ago abandoned his home in Pharaoh's palace, and after that abandoned his home in Midian. For Moses, satisfaction does not ultimately come from a mission accomplished, from that final march into Canaan. It comes from obedience to God.

Among his final words to the Israelites, in Deuteronomy 30:20: "The Lord is your life."

FIVE
WORTH

See, I have engraved you on the palms of my hands....
–Isaiah 49:16a

Miranda was in year three of her job at a Christian organization. The staff was large at her site, with many employees whose work overlapped with hers. At the beginning of her time there, she had been excited about the job, looking forward to shared vision with co-workers and a vocational pull to their joint effort.

But shortly after her arrival, she perceived animosity from one of her colleagues. At first she thought she was imagining it, that she was misinterpreting good intentions. But as the months went by, the animosity became more evident, occasionally surfacing in small but angry bursts from this person, directed at her. Miranda was confused but open to the possibility that she herself had offended in some way. Sadly, her efforts toward resolution went nowhere: her colleague responded with impatience, unfounded accusation, and more anger.

Miranda tried other recourse, carefully seeking advice from a few trusted people who knew them both. She sought help from her boss a time or two.

But busy-ness, combined with the leadership's effort to encourage resolution without finding fault with either party, left the problem unanswered. Meanwhile, a constant tension underlay Miranda's work hours; and occasionally, unpredictably, she continued to be met with hostile, angry, and sometimes accusatory interactions with this colleague.

Quitting seemed the only available solution, but Miranda also needed the income. Daily when she came home from work, she sat on her sofa with her Bible open to the Psalms, finding comfort there and also asking God for deliverance.

She wasn't surprised but was definitely somewhat dismayed when she perceived a response from him: he was asking her to love this colleague.

Then Miranda realized that she did not love this co-worker, that this woman was actually the last person in the world she wanted to love. Miranda spent her days doing her job while also trying to remain at a discreet distance from this colleague. Loving her, by contrast, would mean willing engagement with her. It might even mean seeking her out.

She decided that obedience to God would be nothing short of dangerous, and she really wasn't interested.

Over the days and weeks, this conversation continued: Miranda asking God for help and deliverance, God countering that she needed to love her enemy, Miranda counter-countering that loving her enemy was both impossible and a terrible idea.

And then a new realization: the only way she would be able to love this enemy was if Miranda knew that God loved *Miranda*. The terrible risk he was requiring would only be worth it—or even possible—if he loved her.

The strange thing was that Miranda had been told almost all her life that God loved her, but this was one of the first times that it really seemed to matter.

• • •

Often enough, trusting God feels like a terrible risk. Why take our hands off the controls and rely on someone we can't see? And when waiting, why give up our expectations for the vague and undefined hope that means expectancy?

He told my aunt, "I will never give you anything more than myself." So he also told Paul, who in turn tells us, "And we know that in all things God works for the good of those who love him, who have been called according to his purpose" (Romans 8:28).

But what of those times when the wait seems beyond enduring any longer? When the pain is simply too much? Then, like Miranda, we need to know who we are dealing with. What is this love on which we throw all our hope?

I think that learning God actually loves us is a lifelong process. I became a Christian when I was thirteen. I'm forty-eight now, and sometimes I still think I'm just beginning to believe it.

• • •

Throughout his gospel, John makes frequent reference to one he calls "the disciple whom Jesus loved."

In John 13: 23 "...the disciple whom Jesus loved" was next to Jesus at the Last Supper. In 19:26, "the disciple whom he loved" was standing nearby at his crucifixion. John 20:2 tells us that he was one of two to learn from Mary that the tomb was empty, and in 21:7, this same disciple was the first to recognize Jesus when they saw him, resurrected, on the beach.

Finally, and in what I find to be a rather delightful "reveal" at the end of the book, John writes that this is "the disciple who testifies to these things and who wrote them down" (21:24). In other words, John basically says, "*I'm* the disciple whom Jesus loved."

Does this mean that he was the only disciple Jesus loved? Clearly not. He had endless patience with

Peter, profound grace for Thomas, evident delight in Nathanael—and that was upon first meeting him. And then, of course, there is his own admission of his love for them: "My command is this: Love each other as I have loved you. Greater love has no one than this, that he lay down his life for his friends" (John 15:12-13). He speaks these words to them hours before his arrest.

No, I think John identifies himself as the disciple Jesus loved because John grasped it. He understood that Jesus loved him such that he defined himself, throughout his gospel, in precisely and only those terms.

• • •

Sometimes we might take God's love for granted. Especially in the West, where we enjoy so much in the way of comfort; and especially among those of us who enjoy privilege, we may not make time to appreciate the graces of his love.

Yet these graces frame our world. The powers of reason and curiosity, the love for life and beauty—these among so many others sustain us as individuals and as societies.

To an extent, things are so *right* with the world that they are beyond notice. Maybe it takes a saint or a poet to open our eyes.

• • •

Gerard Manley Hopkins' poem "As Kingfishers

Catch Fire" celebrates these graces, most specifically the one that might be the humblest: the grace of mere *being*. He exults in the very existence of both animate and inanimate objects: kingfishers and dragonflies, bells and even stones that ring out as they are dropped into wells. Hopkins praises the fundamental being-ness, if you will, of each thing as it behaves or functions according to its nature or design. In so doing, Hopkins says, each thing declares itself: "*What I do is me: for that I came.*"

In the second stanza, Hopkins turns his attention to people. They, too, he says, have a purpose, evident when they act justly or are gracious. The poet seems to claim that humankind, acting according to its design, also makes a declaration—but it is not so much a claim of self as it is a claim of Christ. I wonder if Hopkins had in mind Paul's words in Acts 17:28, that in Christ "we live and move and have our being."

Ultimately, the poet helps me see the love God has for me, for us. He declares that the beauties of Christ are manifest in "ten thousand places," in the "limbs" and bodies, the "eyes" and faces of all people. His remarkable finish: that this beauty, seen in the form of every individual in the human population, is beautiful to God because in each one God sees his Son.

• • •

But maybe even that's too general. "God loves you" might be the most resoundingly amazing and fundamental truth in the world, but it's also painted on posters that are then dangled in the background of televised football games or tacked via bumper sticker to the rear-ends of cars. I need to know he loves me in the Specific, if you will: when the entire world seems to have moved ahead without me; when the pending, potential loss sends me reeling. Or when I'm standing in the check-out line at the grocery store.

This is another kind of waiting, one that you may never have noticed, but one that hits me—more or less—every single time I shop.

It's that moment between the ringing-up and carrying my bags out of the store, the moment after I've swiped the debit card and I'm waiting for the word "approved." Here's why: sometimes, when due to job loss that isn't your fault; when your beloved husband has worked hard to piece a steady income together; when the income is sporadic but the bills never are, there simply isn't enough money in the bank account.

You yourself might not know this in the moment. Grocery cart full of groceries and five people to feed at home, you don't realize in the instant that the mortgage came due last night and that the automatic payment went through (thank God!).

What you know instead is the painful "insufficient funds" glaring at you from the card-scanner, or the kind soul who has rung up your groceries finding a gentle way to tell you that you'll be needing a different charge card.

You may have another card, or maybe you don't—but more than once, the upshot for me has been this: sudden heat in my face and a stiffening that seizes my trachea and lungs, accompanied by a new and appalling awareness of the clerk and anyone standing behind me in line. Simultaneously, my mind races to figure out how I can fix this: produce a card that will in fact cover the groceries, pick through my groceries to find only the things I most immediately need (and can afford), or simply (oh, how I've wished for this) disappear.

The first time this happened, I was shopping with my baby daughter. She wasn't yet two years old, and we had chatted happily together as we made our way through the store. In the dairy aisle, I added to our mound of groceries a large bag of shredded mozzarella cheese.

That was a time that I simply left all of the groceries in the shopping cart. Realizing the money wasn't there, I swept my daughter into my arms and left with only her and my purse. I remember Emma leaning back over my shoulder, a plump arm reaching for the bagged groceries that some obliging clerk would have to return, item by item, to their places in the store.

My daughter cried. She had really been looking forward to that cheese.

• • •

Was God's love enough for me then? Was it adequate to the embarrassment—no, shame—I felt as I drove home? I had asked for resolution, for deliverance, for our wretched dilemma to come to an end. His answer was the yellow light on the traffic signal, the inscrutable meaning of "Wait," and while the problem of the bank account wasn't the sum of our need, it was certainly symbolic of all of it.

Did he love me then? Does he love, now, the husband for whom this story and others like it is deeply painful? Who has since then tucked an "emergency hunny" into my wallet so that this might not ever happen to me again?

Not everyone has a husband like mine, and not every partner or person is able to access an emergency hundred-dollar bill. But everyone needs to know that God is nonetheless worth waiting for, that he will be sufficient to answer the need—even when you've left the mozzarella at the grocery store, even when you don't know how you'll cover your rent. Even when the longed-for baby never comes—or the partner, for that matter. Or when, God forbid, the desperately ill loved one never wakes up.

• • •

He gives us this story to help.

A man had two sons. They were his life, his joy, as children ought to be. They were his namesake in a patriarchal world, a society built on having sons and the honor and legacy they meant.

Of course for the second son, the burden and honor of that legacy meant a good deal less. The older brother would be the one to carry on the name, to receive the bulk of the inheritance. He would also bear the responsibility—but the younger son didn't think about that.

He thought, instead, of himself, of the unnamed injustices done to him as they are done to everyone in any family, no matter how well-meaning the parents are.

This younger son—proud, overconfident, greedy, bored—informed his father that he wouldn't be waiting for his inheritance: he wanted it now. This demand was, in effect, a type of abandonment. It was, in reality, a spoken wish that his father were dead. It was a slap in the face and a gut-punch, a haughty and resounding cry of ingratitude. It was an embarrassment—no, shame— of no small degree to his father.

But his father gave him the inheritance anyway, and the son took off for greener pastures—or, rather, for life in the big city, free from what he might have felt was his father's overbearing presence and his ridiculous rules, and also from his profoundly annoying older brother.

I am guessing you know the story, how this second son, rich and untrammeled, did every single thing he wanted until every single penny was gone—as were his briefly acquired friends, and all the food and all the drink and all the luxury he had enjoyed. Then famine struck, and the only job he could find was one shameful to him: taking care of pigs. But even that meager employment wasn't enough. He was starving, wishing he could eat the pigs' food. No one took pity on him, no one cared.

The story reads that this younger son then "came to his senses" (Luke 15:17). And what were they? They were the realization of how wrong he had been: his cruelty to his father and the repercussions of what he had done. He could no longer assume the position of son in his father's household, but he knew that his kind and generous father cared for his servants, that even the hired staff had more than adequate food.

He decided to go home again—to what had *been* his home—and to throw himself on the mercy of the man he had rejected.

Then the best part of the story: the father sees his son coming when that son is still a long way off. I love to think of it. Why would he have noticed him except that he was always keeping an eye out? It wasn't that he had reason to hope: his son's rejection had been absolute. But love always hopes, you know.

He knew this beloved son so well that he recognized his form even at a distance. He knew, perhaps, the slope of those shoulders, the hang of those arms. The gait that belonged to this lost one even when, once upon a time, he was a little boy.

And the father takes off. He had endured the shame of the loss once before, and now he scorns this embarrassment. Gathering his dignified robes and pulling them up to his knees, he runs to the boy before he even knows what he has to say. He won't hear of hiring him as a servant; he will have him back as a son. He trades the young man's tatters for beautiful robes; he puts shoes on his torn and weary feet.

The wealth with which he adorns this one once lost is immaterial, really. It's symbolic. It's a physical expression of the love of the father—and it's the father's love that matters, that welcomes the son home and shelters and feeds him, that speaks against the resistance of the older brother, that gives this prodigal son dignity and restores his name.

We don't know his name. The story is a parable. But if I were to come up with a name for him, it might— for the purpose of our discourse here—be a read-out on the card-scanner in the grocery store check-out line: Approved.

• • •

This is what Abraham had come to believe: that the approval of God was all that mattered. That's the only way he could do what he did when he and Isaac climbed Moriah. It was the only way he could build his altar, pile the wood, bind his boy: "Abraham reasoned that God could raise the dead, and figuratively speaking, he did receive Isaac back from death" (Hebrews 11: 19).

There is a reason we have these and other tales of fathers and sons in the Bible. Not because the Hebrew society was a patriarchal one—although indeed it was. But because God knew what a child means to her parents, the priceless exceptionality of that one.

God put Abraham to this test because he was trying him, yes, and also to give him—and us—a picture of the joy of loss prevented.

I used to think—before I was a mother, perhaps—that the death of Christ could be somehow minimized. It was only three days before he was raised from the dead. How bad could it possibly have been?

But I hadn't known death's shadow yet, and neither did I know my own children. I have three children now, and there's not one of them I'd be willing to give on behalf of anyone else.

If we want to know God's love for us, then we need look no further than his dying Son: the terrible price exacted by sin, the absolute injustice of this death. The Father who must cast his disapproval on the one with whom he had been so well-pleased, and the despairing cry of the one abandoned. Paul says,

For what the law was powerless to do in that it was weakened by the sinful nature, God did by sending his own Son in the likeness of sinful man to be a sin offering. And so he condemned sin in sinful man, in order that the righteous requirements of the law might be fully met in us, who do

not live according to the sinful nature, but according to the Spirit (Romans 8: 3-4).

The phrase I love the most above? "In order that." He wanted us to be able to meet the "righteous requirements of the law," and the only way to effect that was the sacrifice of a complete Innocent as a sin offering. To say that God here lost everything is accurate—and he did it to purchase you. *In order that* he could exchange your tattered clothes for the finest robes. *In order that* he could put shoes on your feet.

But that wealth is immaterial. It's symbolic. What he wants is to have you belong to him, to name you "Approved." To be your comfort in your waiting, even as he is effecting what is best for you. To have you know, beyond a doubt, that he is your very life.

You may be living in an agony of waiting, but know for certain that the Lord cares about the outcome—and the process—far more than you do. See:

He who did not spare his own Son, but gave him up for us all—how will he not also, along with him, graciously give us all things (Romans 8: 32)?

So let the reason for your waiting *not* be the thing you are waiting for. Let the reason be Him.

Out of the depths I cry to you,
O Lord;
Let your ears be attentive
To my cry for mercy.

If you, O Lord, kept a record of sins,

O Lord, who could stand?
But with you there is forgiveness;
Therefore you are feared.
I wait for the Lord, my soul waits,
And in his word I put my hope.
My soul waits for the Lord
More than watchmen wait for the morning,
More than watchmen wait for the morning.

O Israel, put your hope in the Lord,
For with the Lord is unfailing love
And with him is full redemption.
He himself will redeem Israel
From all their sins (Psalm 130).

• • •

My grandfather knew a trick with traffic lights. Riding in his car in New York City, I was amazed at his ability to communicate with them. We would be sitting at a red light, and eventually he would say,

"Red light turn green or I'll call you Charlie Brown!"

On the instant, the light turned green, and we were on our way.

Sometimes I or one of my sisters tried it, but invariably our threatening command had no impact on the traffic light. It remained red for some time, or it turned green when we had barely opened our mouths. Our grandfather had the timing pegged perfectly.

I was much older when I realized how he did it. He

wasn't looking at the red light at all. He was watching the green light above the adjacent street, waiting for it to turn yellow. When that happened, he could gauge his phrasing just so, making it look like our traffic light was responding to his words.

But of course we thought he was magic.

I imagine everyone who waits would like this kind of power. We wish we could lay a hand on an invisible switch and flip it. In waiting on God, I've found myself looking for some trick. Should I simply pray more, or do some fasting? Maybe I should just be a better person. Would any of that make Him—finally—yield to my desires?

So we definitely don't want to be told *how* to wait, because we don't want to be waiting in the first place. To be told how to wait means the endurance game will persist—and this is precisely what we *don't* want.

Yet that yellow light typically has no visible timer. Moreover, knowing we are waiting because this is what God wants, we also know better (despite our pain or discomfort) than to try to rush things.

And so—no matter how much you don't think you want to hear it—*how* do we wait?

SIX
ASK

Trust in him at all times, O people;
Pour out your heart before him;
God is a refuge for us.

–Psalm 62: 8

The first book of Samuel opens with a woman who is waiting. Hannah, wife of Elkanah, desperately longs to be a mother. We don't know how long she was barren, but we do know that it was years, that over the course of time her husband's other wife produced multiple children, and that Hannah suffered the taunts of this other wife because she was childless.

Finally, Hannah took her request directly to God. At the temple with her husband and his family, she promised God that, if he would give her a son, she would commit the child to the Lord.

It's a powerful scene, with Hannah making enough of a spectacle that she drew the attention of Eli the priest. She was weeping. Perhaps she was swaying. She made no sound, but Eli saw that her lips were moving, and he perceived she was drunk. He was so certain of this, in fact, that he told her—a perfect stranger—to quit drinking.

It's a sad moment, full of judgment. Eli didn't bother asking her questions. He didn't try to discern for certain that she was drunk. He knew nothing of her pain. He had no idea what her silent prayer represented as she pled her case before the Lord. He knew little of the reality of barrenness: his wife had borne him two sons. He didn't know what Hannah endured from her husband's other wife. He made his assumption and ensuing accusation, his words like a broom sweeping her out the door.

As readers, we know that Hannah's husband loved her. It didn't matter to him that she had no children. How many times had he asked her, "Why are you downhearted? Don't I mean more to you than ten sons?" (1 Samuel 1:8).

But Hannah wanted to be a mother. Barrenness was a source of shame in that culture and, in Hannah's home, the cause of constant abuse. So she takes her request to God himself. That day, her prayers interrupted, she turns to the accusing priest and explains herself: "I am a woman who is troubled in spirit. I have drunk neither wine nor strong drink, but I have been pouring out my soul before the Lord. Do not regard your servant as a worthless woman, for all along I have been speaking out of my great anxiety and vexation" (1:15-16).

I think Eli repents of his harsh words to Hannah. He certainly accepts her explanation, says a blessing over her, and hopes with her that God will answer her prayer.

And God does: the Lord gives Hannah a son, the child who grows up to be the great prophet Samuel.

And surely this prophet is in God's plan. This is the one through whom God directs the formation of the kingdom of Israel, and he is the one who anoints David king. Yet we see his mother pleading for him before he is born; he is the baby who is the answer to his mother's prayer.

Why does this matter to our conversation? Because here we see that Hannah matters. God could have brought about the life of Samuel in any way he chose, but he did so through a woman who waited and asked for him. The meta-narrative is the kingdom of Israel; but another, smaller narrative is here, too: a woman, waiting for a child, asks God to bring an end to that waiting.

God says yes, and the story is recorded for all time.

• • •

Give ear to my words, O Lord;
consider my groaning.

Give attention to the sound of my cry,
my King and my God,
for to you do I pray (Psalm 5: 1-2).

• • •

Asking comes naturally to us. In most cases, "asking" is the first thing we do in life. You know this if you've spent time in a delivery room: the baby is eased from his mother's body and releases the cry that everyone in the room has been waiting for.

What is that cry if not a question, if not an immediate request for comfort, for warmth, for security? The newborn asks immediately—and we breathe a sigh of gratitude, because this cry also means healthy lungs and indicates a stimulated, well baby.

And babies go on asking, wordlessly crying out for food, for comfort, even for sleep. Grown into toddlers, their cries might turn to shouts or screaming, but most of the time these sounds are nonetheless a form of asking: Please, may I eat? Or How dare you take that from me?

Young children can drive their parents to distraction with all the asking they do, whether they want to know if they can have a snack or they are wondering why the sun is hot. Sometimes it seems there is no end to their asking, and it might ease parental frustration to remember what this asking means: dependence, trust, confidence in parents who hear them.

It's good to be reminded too, then, that Jesus tells us to ask. Far from being frustrated by our repeated requests, he seems to want to hear from us. For example, he tells the story of the persistent widow which, worded differently, might go like this:

There once was a town with a wicked judge. He really didn't care in the least about justice. He didn't care about the people of the town, and he certainly didn't care about obedience to God.

There was a widow in the town, too—one who had been treated unfairly. Her only recourse was to seek the help of the judge—and you can imagine how that went.

But this widow was strong, and she knew she was in the right. She knew the judge's reputation, but that didn't discourage her. Despite his continuous indifference, she continued to ask him for justice.

At first she looked for him where legal matters were decided, but when he refused to hear her, she began to stake him out. She waited for him outside his house; she followed him home from work, she lingered near him at the city gate, always asking.

She drove the judge crazy, and so he caved. He gave her the justice she asked for—not because it was the right thing to do, but because doing so was the only way he could get her to leave him alone.

Then Jesus goes on to say that God, the only truly just judge, will absolutely bring justice for his children who cry out to him for it. Christ says, "I tell you, he will see that they get justice, and quickly" (Luke 18:8).

Jesus tells another story about asking, and this one comes immediately after he has taught his disciples how to pray. The story is less about persistence and more about boldness—and the illustration is, of course, excellent.

He asks us to imagine two friends, one of whom wakes the other in the middle of the night. That is certainly bold, especially when we realize this is not an emergency of, say, health (each of us can imagine waking a neighbor in that case), but rather of hospitality. The friend waking his neighbor has had a guest arrive (at midnight) and has no food to give him.

There is much to be said about hospitality and its value in the near-eastern culture of this story, but what truly matters is the response of the disturbed friend. He basically tells this bread-needy pleader to leave him alone: "Don't bother me," he says.

We might be a little surprised, but that response illustrates the story's theme: the one knocking at the door in the middle of the night is being incredibly bold. In truth, the English Standard Version of the Bible calls him "impudent." The person waking his friend in the middle of the night is actually being rude.

Nonetheless, the friend gets out of bed, unlocks his door, and hands over the bread. Why? Jesus says it's not because the guy is his friend, and not because of the importance of hospitality. It's because his friend was so bold to come asking for bread in the middle of the night.

It's good to recall that Jesus tells this story as he is teaching on prayer. The story is tucked between the prayer he taught his disciples and his words about asking: "Ask and it will be given to you; seek and you will find; knock and the door will be opened to you. For everyone who asks receives; he who seeks finds; and to him who knocks, the door will be opened" (Luke 11: 9-10).

Jesus wants us to ask.

However.

You knew that was coming, didn't you? After all that about expectation vs. expectancy, you can't expect me to leave it there, can you? I want to encourage us to ask *because* Jesus tells us to ask—but we need to remember that our asking never means we get to decide his answer.

Remember me alone in my living room, shaking my fist at the ceiling. I was asking. I was begging. I was telling him in no uncertain terms what we needed. And I think that much pleased him.

That isn't to say that my insistence pleased him—or my anger. But I think he wants us to ask him no matter how we are *feeling*, because the asking means that, in our need, we are having a conversation with him.

When we don't ask, when our waiting builds to a disappointment such that we despair of asking, then we close the door on him. In our frustrated expectation, we shut him out.

There is a better way of asking, one I first heard expressed in a group prayer years ago, before I was a mother, before I had any idea of the waiting my husband and I would endure. I was teaching at a Christian school, and in a faculty meeting one afternoon, we prayed together for something the school or perhaps a family in the school needed.

One among us prayed aloud and said as he did so that we were asking for God to do something, but that we were asking as little children who don't know what is best.

There was such wisdom in this prayer. To pray like children means we can ask with boldness and we can be persistent, but we understand that the outcome—his answer—depends on his wisdom and goodness, and not at all on what we think we need.

• • •

Which of you fathers, if your son asks for a fish, will give him a snake instead? Or if he asks for an egg, will give him a scorpion? If you then, though you are evil, know how to give good gifts to your children, how much more will your Father in heaven give the Holy Spirit to those who ask him (Luke 11: 11-13)!

• • •

My friend Tori thought she knew what was best. In truth, given what she was asking for, I think none would argue that she *didn't* know what was best: she was asking to be delivered from postpartum depression.

Her depression had been severe following the birth of her son. So when her twin daughters were born less than two years later, she was amazed and grateful that it didn't make a reappearance—until the girls were six months old. At that time, her son was twenty months, and Tori was spending her days at home with him and two very needy infants. When the weight of depression settled in, Tori was desperate to get past it.

By nature, Tori is an organized, plan-ahead kind of person. She is great at strategizing in order to get results, and when teaching a class or directing middle or high school students in a play, she gets excellent ones. But anyone who has cared for babies knows that results are long in coming. Adding depression to that equation hobbled her.

Her capacity for planning was among the first of her losses. Far worse was the lassitude that sometimes kept her in bed, unable to care for herself or her children. She felt guilty over the burden she became to her husband and was grieved by her incapacity to work against her depression and serve her family. Efforts with medication didn't work. There was no strategy to mount against this.

Throughout this time, Tori asked God to free her from the depression. She held what she calls "a conversation that didn't feel like a conversation," because, while she was crying out to him in her desperation, he was silent. She says that sometimes she sensed his presence with her, but he gave her no answer.

Meanwhile, the depression was consuming her. It dimmed her motivations, desires and behavior such that she began to forget herself. She compares it to the loss of a loved one when, over time, you might forget what he looked like.

Six months of pleading ensued before Tori perceived some kind of answer, but even then, it wasn't what she was looking for. She wanted to be free of depression, but she was told to fight. God's words to Joshua echoed in her head: "Be strong and courageous!" (Joshua 1:9), and Tori was determined.

Six more months, this time with Tori trying to fight the depression by praising God. Still, nothing worked. The depression would not lift, and new questions came: "What are you doing?" she asked God. "Do you plan to do something?" These, too, were met with silence.

Tori's daughters were two years old when, with yet another new medication, the depression finally eased. She had suffered with severe depression for a year and a half.

She would like to say that she was delighted, and of course Tori was glad and grateful to be well again. But she was frustrated, too. She wanted to regard this triumph over depression as a spiritual victory, she says. She would have liked for her efforts at praise and faithful obedience to have brought the result she asked for.

But she understands now that God had a different answer. Yes, he made her well, but he also wanted her to see that no measure of strategy or effort could make it happen. She says his words to here were these: "You were broken and I kept you in a place of being broken so I could show you that it was me that accomplished this and not you."

Or, as Moses said to Israel, "The Lord is your life."

• • •

Let the little children come to me and do not hinder them, for to such belongs the kingdom of heaven (Matthew 19:19).

• • •

The Israelites grumbled and complained in the desert. They made their desires known to Moses. But they weren't asking. Complaint is talking *at*, not talking *to*. And a complaint, at bottom, is rooted in expectation. It is an assertion of rights, an expression of frustration that one doesn't have what one thinks one deserves.

Asking, by contrast, is born out of humility. It respects the power and wisdom of the one being asked, and it implies submission in receiving an answer. We ask God not because we know what he will do, but because we know who he is. And it, too, is an assertion of rights, but only this right, really: "...to all who did receive him, who believed in his name, he gave the right to become children of God, who were born, not of blood nor of the will of the flesh nor of the will of man, but of God" (John 1:12-13).

Which reminds me, again, of that prayer with the school faculty all those years ago: "we ask you as children who *don't* know what is best."

Oh LORD, my heart is not lifted up;
my eyes are not raised too high;
I do not occupy myself with things
too great and too marvelous for me.
But I have calmed and quieted my soul,
like a weaned child with its mother;
like a weaned child is my soul within me
(Psalm 131: 1-2).

SEVEN
TRUST

You intended to harm me, but God intended it for good.
–Genesis 50: 20

What are you waiting for? Is it a job—or a better one? A spouse who must overcome addiction—or a spouse? A child—or one who needs to be healed? Do you wait for a coworker to be fair to you, a parent to forgive you, an illness to finally pass?

And in your waiting, how often do you feel angry? How many times have you questioned whether this is what you deserve? How frequently are you aware of the terrible injustice that this wait represents?

Much of that sensibility is valid, and sometimes, something can be done. Injustice must be combated, truth must be told. Healing should be pursued; jobs applied for; conversation, at the very least, attempted.

Still, sometimes, we wait.

One of the longest stories of waiting in the Bible comes to us in the latter part of Genesis. Joseph, son of Jacob, might have waited for rescue, for justice, for deliverance—but he never narrates his plight for us; we never overhear his prayers.

What we see is that he learns to trust God.

• • •

Joseph was a spoiled child. The favorite son among twelve, the firstborn son of the favorite wife (among four). This wife had been the only one Jacob had desired, and he had waited for her seven years. When she died an early death giving birth to her second son, the tragedy only cemented Joseph's value in his father's heart: most precious and beloved. He probably looked like his mother.

Living in tents with eleven strapping brothers among three querulous stepmothers, Joseph might have had the good sense to keep his mouth shut, but that particular lesson is one he's long to learn. At seventeen years old he was fool enough to play the tattletale. We don't know what his brothers did, but we know he told on them, and that's all we get of that episode.

Of course his father isn't terribly wise about things either. Living in tents with twelve strapping sons among three querulous wives, Jacob might have had the discretion *not* to make a show of his favoritism—or maybe to reserve such shows for minimal expression: he might have laughed harder at Joseph's jokes, say, or spent a little more quality time with the boy.

Instead, he has to paint his favor in bold relief, a gesture that couldn't possibly be misinterpreted: he makes Joseph a spectacularly beautiful coat. And his son, who may have looked like his mother, inherited his father's good sense and wore that coat whenever he wanted to, which may have been all of the time.

It gets worse.

Joseph has a dream. In it, he and his brothers are binding sheaves of wheat in a field, when suddenly his brothers' sheaves move of their own accord. They circle around Joseph's sheaf and bow down to it.

One would like to think that Joseph keeps this to himself, but remember what I said about silence. At age seventeen, Joseph hasn't learned it yet. Neither has he learned to be sensitive to the feelings of others. He tells his brothers the dream, and they interpret it (how could they not?) as Joseph's prophecy: they will become subservient to him.

They are not happy about this.

Then Joseph has another dream, in which the sun, moon and eleven stars bow down to him.

Again, I think it would have been best had Joseph just kept his mouth shut. Or perhaps he could have left out some of the details (did he have to say *eleven* stars?). In any event, it certainly doesn't help his case with his brothers, who are far more angry with Joseph than he or his father realize.

It's likely that much of the story goes untold. Details of personality and family dynamics are hinted at; the natures of the other brothers are given only rare moments of insight. But we know enough of human nature and sibling rivalry, of family dysfunction and jealousy, to piece it all together. The fact is that the brothers aren't just annoyed by Joseph: they hate him. He is the subject of some heated discussion among them; their shared anger foments into rage. And when they finally see him coming towards them—when they are tending sheep a long distance from their father—this rage is so potent that they decide to kill him.

Between 1926 and 1943, German novelist Thomas Mann wrote a re-telling of Joseph's story. Meticulously researched and compellingly told, the novel fills 1500 pages to narrate those last thirteen chapters of Genesis. While many episodes of Mann's narrative stand out to me, the most vivid is this one: when Joseph comes upon his ten older brothers near Dothan.

Rage is ugly. Its physical expression on the body of another is horrifying. Joseph is seventeen; all of these brothers are older than he; most of them (if not all) are full-grown adults. Ten against one is unfair in any scenario, but here the violence is deeply personal. In Mann's retelling, each of the brothers is eager for his turn, pummeling him with fists, tearing him with teeth.

Joseph is blindsided, uncomprehending, and pleading for his life.

Miraculously, the eldest brother Reuben sees fit to spare the boy's life; the brothers yield to him and, in the end, they sell him into slavery and convince their despairing father that his favorite son is dead.

Thus begins for Joseph a life lived in exile among the Egyptians, a people who fostered a deep mistrust for anyone from Canaan. In fact, there existed strong racial tension between them. In Mann's retelling, we observe that Jacob's family viewed Egypt as a land full of wickedness: where Jacob was Israel, a fledgling nation chosen by and serving the one true God, Egypt was a nation of many gods, their Pharaoh himself among the pantheon.

Jacob and his family knew the Egyptians as pagan. The boy Joseph, doomed to live among them, would be utterly corrupted. He was a son of Israel and a member of God's chosen people, but Joseph's identity in Egypt would be completely erased.

Then Jacob tore his clothes, put on sackcloth and mourned for his son many days. All his sons and daughters came to comfort him, but he refused to be comforted. "No, he said, "in mourning will I go down to the grave with my son." So his father wept for him (Genesis 37: 34-3).

Joseph, captured, purchased, and trundling toward Egypt in the hands of Ishmaelites, had no recourse whatsoever.

One can't argue that he was innocent. He was very

certainly an insensitive tell-all. But it wasn't his fault that the beloved wife was his mother; he wasn't to blame for his father's favor. And no one can be blamed for one's age, either: Joseph was only seventeen. None of what happened to him was commensurate with his foolishness.

Still, we can and must learn from him. Like Hannah and the widow, we must watch what he does. But unlike those of the women, Joseph's story is a long one, and the behavior we trace is less observable. For example, we never see a conversation between him and God. We never witness him crying out for justice. On the other hand, we see further injustice, a long trend of obedience, and God's favor establishing and blessing him at many turns.

Purchased by the captain of Pharaoh's guard, Joseph quickly rises to become head over Potiphar's house. Falsely accused of attempted rape by Potiphar's wife, he is thrown into prison.

When he is placed in charge of all the prisoners, he interprets the dreams of fellow inmates, both of them members of Pharaoh's household. He asks one of these to bring him justice when he gets out, but the man forgets to pursue it, and Joseph sits in prison for two more years.

Then he is called to interpret the Pharaoh's dreams. The king not only receives the interpretation, he also sees the discernment of the interpreter, and soon Joseph is second in command over what was at the time the western world's greatest empire. He saves Egypt from famine, and people from surrounding nations come to Egypt and to Joseph himself, hoping for deliverance from starvation.

Among the masses hoping for assistance? The ten brothers who sold him away.

Joseph is forty years old.

But God sent you ahead of me to preserve for you a remnant on earth and to save your lives by a great deliverance (Joseph, Genesis 45: 7).

There they were, his ten older brothers. Only Benjamin had remained at home. Joseph would have recognized them from a distance as Canaanites: these robed figures would have worn heavy beards. But during the famine, Canaanites were coming to him all of the time.

Perhaps it was when they stood up, straightening themselves after bowing, that Joseph knew their faces: Reuben, Judah, Simeon, all of them. All ten of his older brothers, standing there at his mercy.

They have no idea who he is. That he might be Joseph is the furthest possibility from their minds. They are weary, desperate, and hungry, afraid for their families' lives, for the life of their yet grieving father. This man standing before them, dark and shaved, wearing only thin linen around his waist and dark make-up around his eyes, is—to their minds—an Egyptian and the means to their end: they will give him their silver; he will give them some grain. They will go home.

Here is where Joseph should give vent to his anger and seize some justice. Here he can easily get his revenge. If he commands their lives be taken, it will be done in an instant, and no one will be the wiser. Jacob himself might not miss them very much.

So we watch him carefully. It's the story's climax. After all our hero has endured in exile, here is answer to the attack in Dothan. Instead he plays an elaborate trick, one that is many months in its full execution. Joseph has learned to hold his tongue and to make good use of his advantage. It isn't until he has his brothers in Egypt a second time—their brother Benjamin in tow— that Joseph lets him know who he is.

He has his attendants clear the room so that he is alone with his brothers, "And he wept so loudly that the Egyptians heard him, and Pharaoh's household heard about it" (Genesis 45:2).

These are not tears you dab at, springing to the corners of your eyes and disappearing behind a smile. These are tears that come from the bottom of the soul, joy and grief blended together. This is wailing; these are years of pent-up sorrow. And also, perhaps, they are Abraham's tears as he descends the mountain with Isaac, and Mary's in the garden on that Sunday morning, because soul-shriving, unpredictable and unimaginable joy can do that to you.

Why? Because in Joseph there is no bitterness. There is no claim to revenge. Joseph is only happy and grateful to be reunited with his brothers. In fact, the trick he played was only to make the reunion more complete: Joseph wanted Benjamin to come so that he could be sure his father Jacob would eventually follow.

Joseph is all joy.

For the purposes of this book, this chapter, we have to ask ourselves *How?* How did Joseph arrive here with a heart so fully intact after so many years of waiting? How—after abuse, enslavement, exile, injustice, imprisonment, all caused or incited by the men before him—does he take them in his arms? Yet, "Come close to me," he says.

One might argue that it's his many successes. Sure, he's suffered loss, but look where he is now! Governor of Egypt, father of two sons. A new identity, to be sure, but an identity of great power and distinction. The whole world bows at his feet.

Except that success doesn't do that. Success does lots of things, but it is indifferent to a tender heart. Success is a trapping, an external condition. It is, in truth, immaterial.

Joseph knew success, but he knew it in the way of the prodigal son on his return home. Success was Joseph's second coat. It was given him by his Lord and God, and what it meant to him was his Father's approval—which, as we know, is the only thing that matters.

If you are waiting and you are reading Joseph's story,

you have to watch him carefully. See how he never becomes bitter, how he doesn't stew in his anger. How the injustices done to him become reasons for trusting God, how his obedience—in rejecting Potiphar's wife, in rejecting credit for interpreting dreams—shows us Whom he trusts.

We don't see him at prayer. We don't watch him profess unwavering faith. But Joseph trusts God absolutely; through Joseph and in him, God is at work.

See him there, embracing his brothers, asking about his father, forgiving—even dismissing—the wrongs his brothers did to him. See how he gives all credit to God, how in his waiting he has released all expectation such that he perceives the deliverance when it comes.

In this moment, we only recognize Joseph because it's his story we've been following. But given different conditions—a New Testament beach, maybe, or a waking Jerusalem garden on some eternal Sunday—we could conceivably, for a moment, perhaps, mistake him for Jesus. And that's because Joseph, in these moments with his brothers, looks so like him.

Lesson number two in how to wait? Trust Him.

And we know that in all things God works for the good of those who love him, who have been called according to his purpose. For those God foreknew he also predestined to be conformed to the likeness of his Son, that he might be the firstborn among many brothers (Romans 8: 28-29).

EIGHT
PRAISE

*to speak of
the divine*

*is to draw a circle
around a picture*

*of a pond
and swim*

–Christopher Janke, "Pond Psalm"

The worst kind of waiting? The one that begins with death. You must learn to live in the void she leaves, and you wait—if you are a Christian believer—for reunion.

I have lost loved ones, some more untimely than others—but I think the worst kind of loss is the death of one's child.

My grandfather, the one with the trick of the

traffic light, told me once that I mustn't die before my parents. He was an optimist, a practical man not given to philosophising or dwelling on the dark. And so this remark he made stands out to me. It struck me then and strikes me now as something virtually uncontrollable. Yet, "It's wrong for a parent to have to bury her child," he said.

Such grief would be the worst kind of waiting.

A friend, herself enduring that terrible wait, told me a way she tries to cope with it. The method had been shared with her by another friend whose own child had died: she told herself this life goes quickly. And doesn't everyone say that? My, how time flies—and before you know it, you're celebrating your fiftieth birthday; you're retiring from your job.

So this grieving mother reminded herself that although the wait seemed long, it would go fast. It would be soon that she would see this beloved one again. She had the child's picture framed in a prominent place in her house, one she passed multiple times a day. And as she passed the photo, she would each time say to this one she waited for, "I'll see you in fifteen minutes."

• • •

Waiting is a kind of suffering. I'm careful saying that, knowing that the suffering my husband and I sustained as we waited for meaningful work and steady income is nothing like the suffering of a grieving parent, or one who is desperately ill, or one enduring loneliness.

But all waiting is suffering nonetheless. It's being trapped in the pouring rain outside the train, staring at passengers comfortably seated inside. It's being childless when your arms ache to hold your own baby. It's being packed in a slave caravan to Egypt. It's a kind of exile.

And yet you see that the title of this chapter is "praise."

It makes sense to us, when waiting, that we should ask God for deliverance. It's a stretch—and a lesson—that we should actively practice trusting him.

But praising him is the furthest thing from our minds, isn't it? When the compass of our view is pain and need, praising God seems antithetical to all that seems right. When we are suffering, while we are waiting, *before* we see resolution to our need, praising God makes absolutely no sense. It's so completely unreasonable, the thought should never occur to us. It's like walking on water, really. No one should even consider it.

• • •

When clear rationale is difficult to come by—as it is here—then perhaps we can turn (again) to a poet? That's my go-to, anyway—this time to Christian Wiman.

But I'll admit that his "A Good Landscape for Grief" is a puzzle to me. I've read it dozens of times, copied it out in my own handwriting, underlined and bracketed phrases, made notes to myself in the margin. To anyone who is a real poet, like Wiman or Janke, it's probably not cool of me to try to pin down meaning like this. My paragraphs of explanation (or an effort at it) are prosaic insult to such work—but I can't help myself.

Our poet here seems to choose familiar terrain for this "good landscape." He is from west Texas, and here grief is best set in similarly dry and flat territory. In fact, the dryness suits him in his grief: he is past depression, which he describes as a "wet word" that conjures "claustrophobic moss" and "endless dripping." What appeals in this landscape is a symbolic freedom from dwelling on one's own sadness.

Within this context, he imagines himself coming upon a funeral with that dreamlike quality of having no relation to oneself: a funeral "at which you have no reason/to be." He recognizes no one and doesn't know who has died, but does note that, like himself, the mourners are tearless with "eyes too rapt and intent to weep."

The vagueness of the mourners extends to the one who has died: "he is your father/and your son, my mother and my self." Also vague is the sense of time. The one who has died is "this city of instants," and the mourners are to focus on "this one hole in time" against "the tiny eternities/of our minds."

But that hole is significant. It is a specific moment, and next to it stands a specific person—a boy who, also with that quality of a dream, "has our hands" and "is rearranging his face/as if it were clay." The boy's actions seem to unite the theme of vagueness (how more vague can one be than to have one's face rearranged?) with that of time. I wonder if the face's rearrangement signifies aging and thereby the passage of time.

And then this: beside the specific boy and in this specific "hole/in time" we see that "moment" that "opens and opens in the end/of days like a rose."

What is going on here? The "city of instants" is the life grieved at the funeral. Both cities and instants are finite; each comes to a distinct end. But this moment "opens and opens" such that a bee "in all its hirsute specificity" (again in contrast to the dreamlike vagueness) crawls into it, "its feelers feeling everything as it slowly crawls inside/and never comes out."

I can't get past this bee, its "hirsute specificity." What a splendid phrase! Is the bee the person lost? All of the unique traits and characteristics that made him who he is, and he crawls into the rose, lost to view, never to return?

I think so. We must recall that this is grief's better landscape. The one who has died is "this city of instants," moments of a life, of interaction with this one and that who mourn him. The funeral marks the moment when this loved one disappears from us forever.

But am I wrong to think that Wiman introduces another thought here? Not one that negates the sense of loss, but one that—to borrow his word—opens another sense with it? The end of the poem is a suggestion: this moment of death, of funeral grief, this "end of days" is not a closing but rather an opening, one that "opens and opens"? Does the bee disappear into the rose forever because it has found more life inside?

• • •

Clouds and thick darkness surround him;
righteousness and justice are the foundation of his throne (Psalm 97:2).

Part of what should elicit our praise of God is his otherness. His very eternality, that he is Alpha and Omega, that time does not bind him—these truths of who he is both defy and inspire our understanding.

Poets and artists can sometimes do a better job than the rest of us at showing what is so difficult to say: that there is more than this life, infinitely more. That although we cannot see the God we praise, he nonetheless *is*, and this gives such hope in our waiting.

• • •

In 2015, Hilary Siber was visiting friends in Bangalore, India, on a travel grant. A graduate student in painting, she planned to be there for a month, doing visual research in preparation for her thesis.

She had been in the country for a few hours when she learned that her father had died. He was only 63.

And so Siber found herself reversing the trip she had just undergone, confronting the earliest hours of her worst grief while navigating airport terminals and runways. In retrospect, it was an unavoidably clear parallel: as a Christian, she believes that this life—enclosed in this universe on this earth—is not the end of living. This earth and life are, in truth, liminal spaces, like that of airport terminal and tarmac. An airline terminal serves as segue to our destination; so too this brief life opens onto eternity. And Siber's father, an earnest Christian, had gone to eternity and was more alive than ever with Christ.

Now in some of her work, we see the fruit of that parallel, perhaps most vibrantly in her painting *Further Up, Further In.* The oil painting is far wider than it is tall, and both peripheries are crowded with recognizable if disjointed scenes of daily life. Above each side is a clear yet crooked horizon; and the scenes themselves are somewhat ruptured transitional spaces: parking lots, a runway marked in yellow paint, even the roof of a train platform's waiting shelter.

These distinct, everyday spaces suggest movement. The paint here is slightly smudged and, at first pass, we find we were anticipating this. After all, these spaces imply transit; motion makes sense. But a second study shows us otherwise. In the painting's center, the canvas is almost empty. Bright and blurred, with lights that appear to be in motion, we can't make out any firm objects. Instead, it's as if we are looking into the light itself. Suddenly we understand that the blurred and moving peripheries have almost been pushed to the sides by the light in the center.

Despite the colorful recognizable content of the painting's edges, the eye is drawn to that bright core. Siber has painted her experience since the loss of her father. At his death, she began her wait to be reunited with him. Indeed, her longing for union with Christ himself has continued to increase since that death. And yet she lives here, grounded in the liminal space that is this world. Thus her painting represents her hope in what she cannot see, even as she lives out her present life in what she can see.

• • •

And these are but the outer fringes of his works;
How faint the whisper we hear of him!
Who then can understand his power (Job 26:14)?

• • •

When I was about ten years old, I remember overhearing my mother giving my father bad news. It didn't affect us; it was about some family friends. They lived ten hours away; the wife, Jane, and my mother had been friends in nursing school, and now our families kept in touch, seeing each other about once a year.

I think we were sitting down to dinner when my

mother said that Jane had called. "Norbert lost his job today," she said—and even at my young age I felt a dull dread. Such a thing had never happened to my father; I don't know that I'd ever heard of it happening to anyone. But in that moment, I was aware of some fearsome undercutting, a floor or foundation ripped out from under these friends of ours, and I thought how awful it must be. They had four children.

I don't remember how my father responded, but my mother went on to tell him Jane's response to her husband's very bad news: "Praise God," she had said.

When my husband lost his job in 2001 and again in 2009, those words came back to me. In both cases, the news of our loss felt like shipwreck and abandonment, and praising God did not mean that Bill's job loss was fair or good. Instead, it meant affirmation that God was greater than our losses, that he cared about us in our fear and despair, and that we would see his goodness to us in the midst of this loss and any others that might come about because of it.

Though you have not seen him, you love him; and even though you do not see him now, you believe in him and are filled with an inexpressible and glorious joy, for you are receiving the end result of your faith, the salvation of your souls (I Peter I: 8-9).

Still, how are we to do it? How can we praise what we cannot see, especially when—as in waiting and suffering—what we *can* see is pain, disappointment,

136

loss? Indeed, how are we to trust him? How can we ask him for anything? Observe again the white space in Siber's painting. In conversing with me about it, she herself called the canvas here "empty," because it represents the unknown, the beautiful beyond that we are promised and believe in, but cannot grasp.

Hidden within it is the source of the light, the very Light himself, the Lamb who is the light of the City of God.

He is the image of the invisible God, the firstborn over all creation. For by him all things were created: things in heaven and on earth, visible and invisible, whether thrones or powers or rulers or authorities; all things were created by him and for him. He is before all things, and in him all things hold together (Colossians 1: 15-17).

Among many things, these verses say to me, "You want to see God? Look at his Son." I take this as excellent advice. All right, then. Two scenes *not* taken verbatim from scripture, but *imagined*. Perhaps they went like this:

All of them are tired. It had been an exhausting day, if one finds crowds exhausting. And these crowds were the hungry kind, pressing in, eager. They couldn't seem to get enough of Jesus.

Scale alone here is a remarkable thought, as the crowd numbered 5000—which means that the size was more in the neighborhood of 10,000 or more, if some women also were there (likely) and brought children (also likely). This number had become a source of real frustration to the disciples when appetites turned to eating, as everyone—including the disciples—needed to eat. And then the miraculous: given five loaves of bread and two fish, Jesus fed them all. Afterward, the disciples gathered up twelve baskets of leftovers.

So it was in a post-crowd, continued-amazement fatigue that the disciples obediently boarded the boat. Jesus said to go on ahead of him, and the twelve were relieved by the boat's boundaries: there was just room enough for twelve, maybe thirteen. Okay, maybe more, but none of the 5000 would be joining them, and this was fine. They didn't talk with one another much: the crowds and even the miracle had run them dry. Each was lost in his own thoughts.

It grew dark and the wind increased. Water smacked and slapped against the boat, and the disciples focused on the needs of sailing. Then a disturbing apparition, distant and low on the water. Too small to be another boat, growing larger as it neared them. Soon all of them were watching as it disappeared and then reappeared again above the waves.

Thoughts of the day behind them dissolved in the sea as each disciple, gripped with terror, also clutched the boat. Despite the wind and water, this thing was coming straight toward them, utterly unaffected by weather. They were terrified. One of them cried out, and then another and another, unable to contain the terror: "It's a ghost!"

And then it spoke to them—he spoke to them. "It's me," he said. "It's only me." Was he laughing? "Don't be afraid," he said, his voice coming to them as though he were in the boat, conversational and close. Still smiling, he looked up at the dark sky, down at the white-caps that curled under his feet, and then back at his stunned friends who stared at him, wordless.

He laughed again, delighted. "It's me!" he said again.

That was the night Peter tried it. Peter: bold or foolhardy, depending. "Lord, if it's you, tell me to come to you on the water." Of course it was Jesus! There he stood, beaming at them. Who else could it be?

"Come on!" he said, all joyful encouragement. He stooped and cupped some water in his hand, made to throw it at them, laughed again.

The wind and the waves didn't stop for him, but Peter nonetheless climbed out of the boat. How strange to watch that wet and curling surface sustain him, the water bearing him up as though it did this every day, as if it cared for him somehow, offering to be a home as much as the land is. Peter took a cautious step.

The disciples were transfixed on Peter. Maybe only one of them—was it John?—glanced for just a moment at Jesus who stood, arms akimbo and face alight, grinning at his friend.

When Peter went down, Jesus was there immediately. Distressed for their suddenly sinking friend, none of them saw Jesus cross the pitching yards of water, but there he was, gripping Peter by the upper arm. He wasn't laughing now. "You have such little faith, Peter," he said. "Why did you doubt?"

Later, Peter sat hunched on a thwart, his damp head covered with a dry robe. It was Matthew, seated on the stern nearby, who saw it—or maybe it's just me who pretends it in her mind's eye, because I have known such grace: how Jesus set a hand on Peter's cloaked head and for a moment vigorously rubbed it. Then he clutched robe and some hair together in his fist, turned Peter's face up to his, and grinned at him.

• • •

The woman was a complete disgrace, her clothes were dirty and stained. She had scrounged to find some clean ones, but even the best she still owned were pitiable.

Yet no one pitied her. It was her own fault. They wouldn't have let her near them on any other day— they never did. The stink was enough to ward them off. Even if they didn't know that contact with her would contaminate them, they wouldn't go near her because of the smell. Or the sin. The sin that would infect them would be worse.

But on this day, Jesus was in town, and her desperation—already twelve years old—got the better of her. Here was a chance, she thought, a last and only hope.

The crowd's eagerness protected her. As she pressed in among them, those who bothered to look at her only turned their faces away again. They gave her just an inch of margin and went back to their focus on Jesus.

She caught sight of him in the midst of the crowd and fixed her gaze. People came and went between them, but she was locked in on his back, his cloak, keeping it in her sights. She didn't need to speak to him, didn't need to ask. She had heard he'd cast out demons. If people could become contaminated by touching her clothes, could she not become well by touching his?

There again was a space, an opening, and now he was close enough. She reached through the crowd, between the elbows of two men in front of her, and for a brief second she grasped the rough fabric of his robe.

She needed nothing more. Within a heartbeat, before she released a breath, she knew she was well. The sensation was completely foreign, and yet she knew it: a strength in her core, the sense that the leaking blood had stopped. The weakness, light-headedness, aching were all gone.

For a moment she stood still and upright in the crowd, overcome by the change. And then she knew she had to get out of there.

Threading her way back through the crowd, she kept her head down. The people maintained their almost imperceptible distance, but even this retreat was dangerous: they would note that now she moved away from Jesus. When somehow, someday, they discovered she was well, everyone would know what she had done: touched the master, sullied and contaminated him.

She hadn't gotten far, still hadn't reached the crowd's outskirts when she felt the sea change: something had shifted. Instead of the pressing movement toward the teacher, the crowd had stopped. They were poised, waiting. Voices had quieted, people were looking around.

She heard an unfamiliar voice, confident and quiet, even low—for all it wanted to be heard. "Who touched my clothes?" he said.

Where once her core had been exhaustion and pain, now it constricted with fear. If they found her out, they might kill her for this. Everyone knew who she was. Her condition was no secret. The teacher would get hold of her; the conversation would be swift. She would be dead within the hour.

She had to get out of there, but in the crowd's new stillness, any movement would be noticed. Her only hope was to keep her head bent, eyes down. Stay still.

There was conversation. Some people were talking. The crowd was beginning to loosen, as if some people were making room for others. Two men brushed past her now, quickly, and she heard one mutter to the other,

"Who *touched* you? *Everyone* touched you, that's who," and she felt a momentary relief.

But still she heard the voice and with it felt the crowd ripple outward. "Who touched me?" he said again. "Who touched me?"

She wasn't going to get away with this. She knew it. He was coming closer, making a bee-line, but slowly, almost as if he knew where she was. "Who touched me?" he said again, but the words weren't angry ones. He was almost quizzical in his asking, as if this were a game. But it wasn't. She began to shake.

"Who touched me?" again, so close to her now, and the voice was kind, but she couldn't bear for him to find her.

Without thinking, she pushed past the woman who stood between them just as Jesus slowly turned toward her. She collapsed at his feet, head bent, her whole body trembling.

"I did," she said.

And then without looking up, she began talking, telling him the whole story, all twelve of the years. The baby she had lost, the husband who had left her, the hovel where she made her life at the edge of town.

She was not the only one amazed when he bent down and then folded his legs so that he sat, so close, in front of her. She didn't dare raise her face to look at him; she was working hard not to cry; and she stopped talking only because she had run out of words and she felt something firm on the top of her head, gently pressing it back to raise her chin, so that she was staring him in the face.

He was watching her, listening, looking at her intently as if he'd loved her for a long time, and also as if there was no one in the world he'd rather listen to.

Just two stories, but "Jesus did many other things as well. If every one of them were written down, I suppose that not even the whole world would have enough room for the books that would be written" (John 21: 25).

What do even these two stories tell us about him? How, in their brief tellings, do they fill in for us the white center of Siber's painting? What do they tell us of the secret interior of Wiman's rose?

What beauties do we see here of God's image? We need to find those truths about him—all of them beautiful—and praise him.

And then, of course, there is this:

"Have this mind among yourselves, which is yours in Christ Jesus, who, though he was in the form of God, did not count equality with God something to be grasped, but emptied himself, by taking the form of a servant, being born in the likeness of men. And being found in human form, he humbled himself by becoming obedient to the point of death, even death on a cross" (Philippians 2: 5-8).

• • •

In the story we call "the prodigal son," we find a second son, one often overlooked. He is barely mentioned at the story's beginning ("a man had two sons"), and the plot for a long time turns on the second one, the one who famously squandered his abundant inheritance in the name of selfishness.

But the elder son is important, too. He is the "good boy," the one who stayed home in apparent fidelity to his father.

Or did he? When his younger brother returns, we see no allegiance in the elder son at all. He is furious with his father, bitterly jealous at the rejoicing and celebration.

At the story's end, it's the father we watch in the closing scene. He is the one who ran to the younger brother, restoring his identity, welcoming him home. And now he stares after his fuming older son, still hoping he'll come to the feast.

This is the God we wait on.

At the end of the day, at the end of history, and even in those thirty-three short years when, incarnate, God broke into the physical world, it's a real and living relationship he wants with us. It cost him his life to bring it about.

We praise him in our waiting because—come what may— he will never give us anything more than himself. Again, what else is there?

Though the fig tree does not bud
And there are no grapes on the vines,
Though the olive crop fails
And the fields produce no food,

Though there are no sheep in the pen
And no cattle in the stalls,
Yet I will rejoice in the Lord,
I will be joyful in God my Savior (Habakkuk 3: 17-18).

Praise is verbalized trust. It's the other side of asking. It's thanking God in advance for his answer, no matter what it is, because our confidence is in who he is and the goodness—again, no matter what—of what he will do.

And praise takes practice. It can be a discipline. It would be nice if it were as natural as breathing, if words of praise came from our mouths as regular exhalation.

But he accepts it in any offering, whether it's recited scripture or something we've composed in the moment, uttered in a moment of genuine gratitude or as a kind of mourning—in a moment of loss or a fresh awareness of how limited we are.

He knows better than we do that praising *him* brings life and peace to *us*, and he is willing to accept it even when, in any number of dark moments, we don't feel at all like we mean it: "Through Jesus, therefore, let us continually offer to God a sacrifice of praise—the fruit of lips that confess his name" (Hebrews 13: 15).

And, happily, praise can be a thing we practice, reminding ourselves to do it as we go along. For while praising God is natural to us, I don't think it necessarily *comes* naturally: we live in exile, after all. Peter might have gotten better at walking on water if he hadn't been busy with other things. I'm guessing that he's excellent at it now.

NINE
WATCH

*And here again is a foreshadowing—the world will be made
whole. For to wish for a hand on one's hair is all but to feel it.
So whatever we may lose, very craving gives it back to us again.
Though we dream and do not know it, longing, like an angel,
fosters us, smoothes our hair, and brings us wild strawberries.*

−Marilynne Robinson, *Housekeeping*

M y father was at home sick, so he kept my little sister with him my while my mother rode her bicycle to the store. It was a ride of fifteen minutes or so, through our little compound of identical houses and then past a system of apartment buildings, around a rice paddy or two and then into town.

She didn't have too much to buy, but she was pleased to have found a broom to add to her purchases. A broom is an unwieldy thing to carry on a bicycle, but she thought she could manage.

Soon enough, however, the broom became a challenge. She had to hold it with both hands across the handlebars, which of course made the bicycle handles almost impossible to grasp. Steering was difficult.

It was one of the only times she wished for a car while we lived in Japan. But wishing for a car at that moment wasn't terribly helpful. So instead, she prayed for a ride—for her broom.

What were the chances? Our compound was small; people weren't doing errands all that often. It was very likely she would find herself pedaling (and swerving) that broom on her bicycle all the way home.

Still, she asked.

And in very little time, someone from our compound came along, stopped at the curb, and very gladly gave our broom a ride home.

It's easy, when waiting (as we have said) to be so fixed on our desires and expectations that we miss things like this. And what is it we are missing? God's kind provision, given again and again. We have to believe that he is good and that he will provide. We have to watch for the provision—and then we get to praise him for it.

• • •

Dr. Allen met us in the parking lot. He was on his way into the gym that morning, and after that his day was packed. At the time he had three children of his own, and I think at least one of them was in tow that Saturday, going to spend the next hour in the gym's playroom while Allen got in a quick workout.

Meanwhile, my youngest was presenting with some disturbing symptoms. I can't remember what they were anymore, don't recall what I couldn't overlook or wait on but instead had to see the doctor immediately. Allen was our doctor, so logically he examined Emma on the curb in front of the gym, and he determined that she was fine.

Allen was a very close friend. He still is—and he served as our children's pediatrician until their mid-teens. When, a few years ago, my middle one split open the back of his head doing a backflip at the swimming pool, we went over to Allen's house to have the staples out. Afterward, Allen handed them to me in a sandwich bag.

Then there was the time that Emma, a toddler, had a terrible case of croup. Allen came to our house to diagnose her and soon enough was riding with us to the emergency room.

He also took care of our eldest when, age ten, Will returned with us from a mission trip to Kenya with disturbing symptoms. I didn't know it at the time, panicked as I was by my son's lethargy and high fevers, but Allen was busy for a while after that, sending Will's blood work all over the hospital, investigating the many frightening possibilities that could accompany one home from a developing nation. Turns out, it was the flu.

And when in a rousing game of Bulldog my husband smacked his head into the pool wall swimming with his eyes closed, Allen glued the cut closed at his kitchen sink.

For the earliest years of my children's lives, we had very limited health insurance. The loss of a convenient pediatrician—who kept all our records on file and would see us at short notice or advise me in the middle of the night for an ear-infection—had been one of my earliest terrors when Bill lost his job the first time.

At the moment of that loss, we had already been in a small-group Bible study with Allen's family and some others for several years. That we were in serious need of a pediatrician was a problem neatly absorbed by Allen. He didn't make a fuss about it, didn't tell me where to enroll the children or announce that he would take care of their needs. But ever afterward, whenever a need arose—or when someone needed a physical for something-or-other, Allen made space for us in his schedule, in his office, or at his kitchen sink. We never had to pay for it.

• • •

Over the many years of our greatest need, we were often helped by others. There were times when it felt like the bottom had completely dropped out—and suddenly a check would come from a friend. There was the series of weeks—I'm embarrassed to say that I don't know how many—that a friend's parents provided us with a weekly gift card to the grocery store.

Often, it seemed like these gifts would come when I'd been feeling desperate. More than once they came after I'd had one of those fist-shaking-at-the-ceiling conversations, those times when I said to God in no uncertain terms, "We live here."

Of course, it was all very humbling. Who wants to be the needy one? To be needy is to sit in the weak seat, to lack agency. And anyway, the scripture reads this way: "It is more blessed to give than to receive" (Acts 20:35). As you might imagine, I complained to God about this, too. I wanted to be the generous one, the one with money. The one to sail in with a meal and some comfort and fix someone else's world for a change.

That was a long lesson, a drill in humility that I still need to rehearse time and again. I know I was definitely learning a thing or two about Christ's body— the Church—and how it is meant to work. Yes, we are meant to serve one another in the body of Christ—but someone has to be willing to be served.

• • •

But we don't want to be in need. We don't want to be waiting, to be in exile, far from home. We don't want to be wanting. We want it to be over with, to learn whatever it is we're supposed to learn, to get out of this discomfort, whatever it may be.

Maybe some of that sounds familiar.

Remember, this is a book about waiting.

• • •

The Israelites had been out of Egypt for one month and fifteen days when some of them summoned their nerve to complain. They went to Moses and told him in no uncertain terms that they were hungry.

In truth, that's not what happened. According to Exodus, *all* of them complained. And they didn't say they were hungry so much as they basically told Moses he never should have rescued them, that they had been better off in Egypt (and enslaved) where they "sat around pots of meat and ate all the food (they) wanted" (16:3).

This is not a good moment for many reasons, but it becomes one of the most mysterious moments I know. In the first place, it's mystifying because of God's mercy in the face of impressive ingratitude. And in the second, it's amazing because of how he provides for his people.

He promises them bread in the morning and meat at night. That very evening, "quail came and covered the camp." And the next morning when they awoke, the ground around their camp was covered in dew. As the sun rose and the dew evaporated, white flakes appeared on the ground that turned out to be bread "white like coriander seed and tast(ing) like wafers made with honey" (Exodus 16:31). They called it manna, meaning "what is it?" because they had never known anything like it before.

This extraordinary provision continues throughout the Israelites' exile in the desert. Their morning and evening meals were delivered fresh daily—with the exception of the Sabbath. The night before the Sabbath, they were commanded to save some for the next day, as God desired that their rest be complete.

And God commanded another thing: he asked that they take a measure of manna to store it. Why? This bit of bread is going to last for generations to come, serving as a reminder to the people that, when they were unable to provide for themselves, God fed them with his own hand.

• • •

"'I tell you the truth, it is not Moses who has given you the bread from heaven, but it is my Father who gives you the true bread from heaven. For the bread of God is he who comes down from heaven and gives life to the world'" (John 6: 32-33).

Here we have yet another extraordinary moment in scripture. The very same crowd whom Jesus had fed with five loaves and two fish comes after him the next day. I think it's fair to say they rather liked the free food that they'd enjoyed and, looking at this man as the might-be Messiah, they decided to hold him to their highest standard: Moses.

They raise the issue of that miraculous manna, telling Jesus that they'll believe in him and live obedient lives if he can just produce for them a miraculous sign. Such as, maybe, I don't know, feeding them. Again.

But as ever, Jesus is doing something more. He is pointing to something bigger, to the white space in the middle of the canvas, to the truth that will satisfy but that, as yet, is not entirely clear to our vision: "I am the living bread that came down from heaven. If anyone eats of this bread, he will live forever. This bread is my flesh, which I will give for the life of the world" (John 6: 51).

Here is our provision. Right here and nowhere else. In this terrible speech—after which many disciples will desert him—Jesus tells us our worth. Unlike the life of Isaac, this Son's life will not be spared. What is difficult to accept and what is tricky for us to keep our eyes on—especially when we are waiting for anything— everything—else is that *this* is what we need.

We may want the baby, the job, a seat on the train. But always he tells us the same thing: we need his flesh and blood, his sacrifice, the death that saves us eternally into a life that opens and opens.

He gave his very life to make it happen, and so everything else that happens also matters to him. But let us remember what he is saying: no matter what we think we want, he is what we long for.

As the deer pants for streams of water,
So my soul pants for you, O God.
My soul thirsts for God, for the living God.
When can I go and meet with God (Psalm 42: 1-2)?

We don't want to be in need or want. We don't want to wait. At the very least, it makes us feel weak. At worst, it means suffering and pain. But see how it directs our gaze to him, see how it helps us see his provision? From a doctor's visit on the parking lot curb to the realization— yet again—that he is the Bread of Life, waiting can lift our chin and draw our gaze from the periphery to the One who is worthy of praise.

There was a time when I began to see it coming to an end. My husband's business began to thrive. We were able to pay off debt. And suddenly my vision cleared. The hard lines of the liminal space that is this world began to swim again into view. I began to realize that my sense of desperate reliance on him would no longer be so acute. For years I had been leaning heavily on him, living in hope of him— and so hadn't been as fixed on this world as I might have. After years of living in dependence, of knowing that I was fed by his hand, it appeared I might think I no longer needed to.

I was—and am—profoundly grateful for the practical relief that my husband's work brings.

But, at the time, I checked myself: If our need were no longer so great, what might I miss? The provision that clearly came from him, the kindness that turned my face to his would potentially be obscured by a regular paycheck. I could see that this might actually be a loss.

Which made me wonder about the Israelites. Among the triumphant and grateful people pouring into the Promised Land after 40 years in the desert, were there some among them who noticed? Who realized that the quail-and-manna-provision had come to an end? Some who, collecting that last bit of manna, bit into it wistfully, knowing that this was the last time?

Our need for him while we wait for him is a precious gift. Let's not squander it.

EPILOGUE

I began this book talking about trains and the very real annoyance I felt when—at five, six, seven years old—my family didn't own a car.

Recently I learned why we didn't have one.

Apparently, before we moved to Japan, my parents set aside money to buy a car. Shortly after we arrived, they began looking for a used one and had the help of a Japanese friend in their search. But soon they learned that our church back in the States was looking to buy a small house. The building was on a lot adjacent to the church, and they hoped to buy it to house the Sunday school.

So my parents sent our car money to help.

In those moments that I complained about *not* having a car, they never offered this explanation. Their decision to send our car money for a Sunday school building wasn't about impressing me or anyone else. It was a gesture of love for that church and for the greater Church that Christ died for. It was a gesture of love for God.

But perhaps you're familiar with this: "We love because he first loved us" (1 John 4:19). When we know that he loves us, it gets easier to trust him—with things like transit, or any means of control, or in the absence of control, that means waiting on him.

"He is a lover, not a train." Trains are good, in their way. Their predictability is very helpful. But God is real and alive, sustaining and rescuing, actively working to deliver and, in the meantime, to show us his love.

While you are waiting, watch for Him. He is coming, and He is already there.

ACKNOWLEDGMENTS

The Old Testament is full of the call to remember. And when, at the Last Supper, Jesus speaks to his disciples—they who will become the Church—he tells them to participate in this covenantal meal in remembrance of him.

We are creatures short on memory. Give us a new potential terror and we tend to lose sight of all of God's goodness, kindness, faithfulness in the past. He gives us his word to combat our fear, and he also gives us each other. We are to remind each other of the promises in scripture, and we are to tell each other the stories of his faithfulness to us.

In light of that, you might imagine how encouraging it was for me, as I researched for this book, to talk with others who have waited and are waiting on God. I am indebted to each of the women who shared her story with me; each represents, in her own way, what it means to watch for and trust in God beyond what we see or realize in a lifetime. My heartfelt thanks to these women for their candor, generosity, and faith.

I especially want to thank Hilary Siber who, not

all that long ago, shared with me a wall between our classrooms, and who for this project so readily opened to me her grief and faith in talking about the loss of her father. She not only shared that story, but also her painting, which truly does the work of a thousand words and then some. I encourage you to seek out her art. Every piece I've seen is worth contemplation.

Thanks, too, to Elizabeth Turnbull, my editor and the first one to read the book in full. She, too, knows what it means to wait, and her encouragement throughout this project has been priceless.

I'm grateful to Jay Thomas who with careful eye, red pen, and hearty encouragement, vetted my initial ideas. And to Malcolm Pettigrew, the second early reader, who deeply encouraged me and also helped me bring clarity to the text where it was lacking.

These acknowledgements wouldn't be complete if I didn't include the many, many friends who have listened to, encouraged, and supported us—with prayer, time, and sometimes financial help—through our long wait. Each of these friends has been part of God's provision to us: Allen and Bonnie Liles, Andrew and Marnie Ginsberg, Christina and Rhett Gibson-Davis, Debbie and Ken Tunnell, Chris and Kim Roberts, Heidi Simonsen, Chip Denton, Brent Clark, Beth Wessels and Eric Rice, Carolyn and Mike Shipley, Daun Whitley, Sonya Hove, Emily Williams, Kathy Russell, Rebecca and Jay Thomas, Annie Hawkins, Malcolm and Kelly Pettigrew, Branson and Cristy Page, Lisa and Jim McConnell, Rachel and Nat Stine, Scott and Lynne Liptak. I suppose I've given myself an out (above) with that quip about faulty memory, but I fear nonetheless that I have forgotten someone. If so, I'm sorry. Know that we remain grateful to you and that our faithful God remembers your kindness.

And deepest gratitude to my husband, Bill. His gift of joy and trust in God throughout the years I've described here made our waiting far more endurable than it might otherwise have been. In truth, his joy taught and still teaches me what it means to have confidence in God's goodness. And his willingness for me to tell our story is a gift of tremendous generosity. I would not have written this without it.

Finally, I'm grateful to my parents, who continue to live in faithful pursuit of our faithful God, and who continue to remind me—through their own stories and lives—that he is indeed coming, and will not delay. Thank you so much, Mom and Dad. I love you.

THE AUTHOR

Rebecca Brewster Stevenson is a native of Pittsburgh, Pennsylvania. She has a master's degree from Duke University and has lived in Durham, North Carolina for over 20 years with her husband and three children.

Though Rebecca's debut novel *Healing Maddie Brees* was published in 2016 to literary acclaim, she has been writing for most of her life. Her beautifully crafted personal essays on her blog "Small Hours" have earned her a strong audience of readers who enjoy her explorations of themes relating to family, marriage, faith, writing, language, literature, and film.

"Rebecca Brewster Stevenson's writing is consistently powerful, complex, honest, and hopeful" (Andy Crouch, author, *Culture Making and The Tech-Wise Family*). Rebecca's writing has also been called "exquisite" (Stephen Chbosky), "thought-provoking" (*Library Journal*, Starred Review), and "gorgeous" (*Kirkus Reviews*).

To connect with Rebecca, visit her online at rebeccabrewsterstevenson.com or follow her on Instagram @rebecca_stevenson17.

ALSO BY
REBECCA BREWSTER STEVENSON

Healing Maddie Brees

a novel

"A gorgeous meditation on broken bodies, fractured faith, and the soul-wrenching path to serenity."

–Kirkus Reviews

Maddie Brees has been given bad news: She is seriously ill. But she also has an old friend, an ex-boyfriend who might be able to heal her. She was witness to Vincent Elander's so-called miracles in the past. But that was a long time ago, a memory that she would rather stay buried.

Now she is happily married to Frank and mother of their three young boys. The religion of her past is behind her, along with any confidence she once had in it. With the onset of her cancer, the memories of Vincent won't leave Maddie alone, and before long they are affecting everything else: her marriage, her husband, the things they thought they agreed on, the beliefs they thought they shared. Soon Frank, who was to be Maddie's rock throughout her treatment, is finding fault-lines of his own. In this exquisitely written narrative, Stevenson explores the questions of honesty and commitment, of disease and isolation, and of the many shapes healing takes.

CPSIA information can be obtained
at www.ICGtesting.com
Printed in the USA
FFHW021800150519
52457859-57868FF